LET'S GET DIGITAL
How To Self-Publish, And Why You Should

David Gaughran is the author of *If You Go Into The Woods*, *Transfection*, and has just released the epic historical adventure *A Storm Hits Valparaiso*. Born in Dublin, he currently lives in Stockholm, but spends most of his time traveling the world, collecting stories.

Praise for *Let's Get Digital: How To Self-Publish, And Why You Should*:

"Let's Get Digital is a must read for anyone considering self-publishing."—JA Konrath, bestselling author of *Trapped*, *Origin*, and *Whiskey Sour*.

"Credible and comprehensive. I'd recommend it to any writer who is considering self-publishing or anyone interested in the current state of publishing."—*Big Al's Books and Pals*.

"Even with my background as an indie writer, I picked up several valuable tips… this is simply the best book about the e-book revolution I have read."—Michael Wallace, bestselling author of the *Righteous* series.

"It should be THE starting point for anyone considering self-publishing today. This book is a Pixel Pick, and should be considered required reading for any Indie author."— *Pixel of Ink*.

LET'S GET DIGITAL

DAVID GAUGHRAN

LET'S GET DIGITAL
How To Self-Publish, And Why You Should
ISBN-13: 978-1475212600
ISBN-10: 1475212607

Editor: Karin Cox
Cover Design: Kate Gaughran
Print Formatting: Heather Adkins

E-book edition published July 2011
Print edition published January 2012

This first paperback edition was printed by Createspace

ArribaArribaBooks.com
DavidGaughran.com

Contents

PART THREE: SUCCESS STORIES

Acknowledgements
About the Author
A Storm Hits Valparaíso (Sample)

Dedication

This book is dedicated to the self-publishing community.

Introduction

This is the part of the book where I am supposed to demonstrate my expertise, list a string of impressive credentials, talk about my years of experience in New York publishing, and wax lyrical about all of the books I have written. But you know what? I can't. Yet I can still publish professional-looking books like the one you're reading right now. And if you keep reading, I can teach you how. The first thing you need to learn is: *anybody can do this.*

If you have the technical capability to operate an e-mail account and download this book, you have the capacity to learn what it takes to become a publisher. That's right—a publisher. Never forget that's what this is: a business. If you adopt a professional attitude and are willing to put in the time, you might even make some money. It's down to you. There are no gatekeepers and there's no-one else to blame if you fail.

I think it's only appropriate that I tell you a little about myself. My name is David Gaughran and I am a 33-year-old Irish writer living in Sweden. I have written a couple of books and several short stories. I spent 18 months sending queries to British and American agents, collecting more than 300 rejections before coming to my senses and taking back control of my life. I still remember the day: Sunday April 3, 2011. The day my life changed forever. The day I decided to become a publisher.

I had been in bed with the flu all week and spent most of the time coming to terms with the changes in the publishing industry. Barry Eisler had just walked away from $500,000 to go it alone, and self-publishing star Amanda

Hocking had just signed a $2 million deal with a New York publishing house. To me, these two developments, while in direct opposition to each other, were *proof* of the bona fides of self-publishing. I started listening to self-published authors, such as Joe Konrath and Dean Wesley Smith, who were showing others their sales numbers, *real* numbers, and urging others to make the leap.

I still wasn't sure whether to self-publish my novel. At that point, I still had some interest from agents and I wasn't sure how it was going to play out. I decided to start off with a couple of short stories, to test the water, and then follow that with a collection. My intention was to see if I made any money and to see how difficult self-publishing really was. I knew I had a lot to learn; what I didn't know was how much fun it was going to be.

This book will teach you how to do exactly what I did: start with nothing and publish your own work to a professional level, then distribute it so that anyone around the world can read it, download it, and pay you for it.

The subtitle of this book is: "How To Self-Publish, And *Why* You Should." That's not just window-dressing. *Part One* gives you an overview of the rapidly changing publishing business. It explains why the big publishers are in serious trouble, how the internet has revolutionized publishing to the point where a writer, working alone, can make a living out of it, and why you don't really need to fear piracy. It shatters the myths surrounding self-publishing, chief among them being that you will never make any money. And it explains why this is a great time to be a writer and how you can profit from the seismic changes that are taking place.

Part Two deals with the nuts and bolts of digital self-publishing. It covers everything from finding an editor, arranging a professional cover, formatting your book so it appears perfectly on every device, coming up with an appropriate pricing strategy, and a host of marketing tips covering everything from blogging, social networking, reviews, competitions, to how to arrest a sales slump.

Finally, in *Part Three*, I present the inspiring stories of 33 bestselling self-publishers, who share their journeys in their own words.

Why I Decided to Self-publish

I've been scribbling something or other since I could hold a pen, but I have been writing seriously for about five years now. It all started with a trip to South America, where an old story from the independence wars hooked me. I started researching the background—just curious—and before I knew it, I was writing a historical novel. It was a monster, and it took me more than three years to write, but it gave me an excuse to go back to South America for another nine months. When I was finally done, I started querying.

I spent 18 months researching agents and sending out submissions, rewriting the novel three times based on feedback. At Christmas last year, I thought all that hard work had finally paid off. An up-and-coming, well-respected New York agent expressed interest in representing me and we spoke twice on the phone. He told me how "in love" he was with my novel, how everyone in his office had read it and loved it, and that it was "big, sweeping and really great." Then he never contacted me again. I found that very disheartening. I couldn't even summon up the energy to start looking for another agent. I was working on a second novel, but I found myself questioning everything. All the joy had gone out of writing.

I had read a little about self-publishing, but it only became a serious option for me in the week that Amanda Hocking signed a big trade deal and Barry Eisler walked away from one. I saw these events as a validation of self-publishing and spent a week tormenting myself, wondering whether I should self-publish my novel or not.

I broke the impasse, deciding to start off with some short stories. I already had some success publishing short stories in magazines and anthologies, so it seemed like a low-risk way to both learn the process and test whether I wanted to do this with my novel. At the same time, I began writing a blog about my journey. Within a week or two, I was getting more than 200 views a day, and feisty conversations in the comments.

After four weeks of manic preparation and very late nights, I released my first e-book. It cracked the Kindle Top 40 Short Story charts on the first full day and picked up some lovely reviews. In the three months since I made my decision to self-publish, I have never worked so hard on writing. Aside from setting up a blog and posting more than 1,000 words a day there, I had to hire an editor, and find a cover designer. I had to learn how to format e-books from scratch and how to sell them.

I found the whole self-publishing process exhilarating. I loved being in complete control of what I could write, what I could publish, and how I published it. I loved having the final say on every little detail, choosing the price, and promoting the book myself. I loved coming up with fun competitions.

But the most gratifying thing was how much my productivity as a writer went up, even with all the extra work I had to do. There is something very motivating about self-publishing. I guess it's knowing that the reader will get to see your work as soon as you are done and they—and no-one else—will decide if it's a success or not. It's very democratic.

So, how did I go about it? I got my sister (a professional cover designer) to do the cover, found a professional editor through a forum, and learned the formatting myself. I wanted to put out a product that looked as good, if not better, than anything coming from large trade publishers, but at the lowest possible cost. I studied how the bestsellers were presented, and I copied them.

Right from the start I decided to blog about the whole process, posting each step as I went. All of the information on what I needed to do was out there, but some of it was hard to find. There was also a lot of misinformation. I wanted to gather all of the correct information in one place so that other self-publishers would find it easier.

Four weeks after I made my decision, my first e-book, *If You Go into the Woods,* went live. Before I even told anyone about it, someone had bought it and reviewed it—that blew my mind! I made 50% of my costs back in three weeks. At that point, I released my second title, *Transfection,* an old-school science fiction short. And, after six weeks, I had sold 200 e-books. Not bad for an unknown, previously unpublished writer. I thought it would take me six months!

On top of that, my blog really took off. I went from zero views a day in April to 3,500 views *a week* in June, with lots of readers deciding to self-publish and follow each step along with me. We all shared information and advice, and it was great to see some of my blog regulars release their writing a few weeks later.

So, should you self-publish? No-one can make that decision for you. But consider this: it's not either/or. There is no reason why you can't self-publish some projects and pursue a trade deal for others. However, before you make any decision, you should learn as much as possible about what is happening to the publishing industry.

My only regret is that I didn't self-publish sooner. I'm having more fun writing than ever before. I'm connecting with my readers. And, best of all, I have made a ton of new friends.

Stockholm, July 2011

PART ONE: THE DIGITAL REVOLUTION

This book won't just tell you *how* to self-publish; it will tell you *why* to self-publish. This section is intended to give you an overview of how radically the publishing industry has changed in the last few years. The internet has revolutionized every single business it has come into contact with, and publishing is no different. The industry has always limped from one crisis to another. But, for the first time, these changes are handing power back to writers.

1. Challenges Facing the Publishing Industry

The publishing industry in the 21st Century is in the throes of some pretty major changes, and the full effects will take years to play out. Hardly a week goes by without distressing headlines. Publishers are downsizing, booksellers are going to the wall; even distributors are feeling the pinch.

Much of the modern-day woes can be traced back to the Great Depression, when booksellers insisted on a returns policy that would allow them to ship back unsold books. This policy kept booksellers (and some publishers) afloat during tumultuous times, but when the economy rebounded in the run up to WWII, and expanded in its aftermath, this policy remained in place, and still exists today. This has had a number of important effects.

It means that booksellers order more copies of a book than they think they will sell—just in case. They know a customer is unlikely to wait for an order to be placed when they can simply buy it elsewhere or go online. Stores can order as many copies as they like (the only restriction being the cost of storage), safe in the knowledge they can return unsold copies. Independent booksellers, which lack the storage capacity of large chains, tend to be more judicious in their buying habits.

Nevertheless, more than half of the books that publishers print are returned. Most cannot be sold again at full price, are tattered or damaged from shipping, and end up being pulped. In Canada alone, an estimated 50 to 100 million books are pulped per year. That's around 600,000 trees, or, to put it another way, more than 200,000 tons of carbon dioxide emitted to produce books that are going to be pulped anyway. Per year!

If you think those numbers are high, remember that the publishing industry in the United States is 15 to 20 times bigger. Even worse, despite rising populations, readership numbers have plateaued, yet more and more books continue to be printed every year.

But what about the cost to publishers? Printing, storing, distributing, and pulping all of those books costs a lot of money. So why do publishers do it? Why not concentrate on fewer titles they are sure will sell? The answer is: because they are terrible at predicting what will be a hit. Books with multi-million dollar advances (and enormous print runs) can tank; the work of unknown authors, with little marketing behind them, can fly off the shelves, leading publishers to rush back to the printers hoping to capitalize on the wave before it subsides.

The truth is, nobody can be sure. Marketing helps, a "name" on the cover helps, a hot genre or topic helps, and good reviews help, but what really sells books is word-of-mouth. Think of your own buying habits. Think of your favorite books and authors. How did you discover them? I bet the majority were friends' recommendations.

Because publishers can't predict what is going to be a hit, they need to gamble on a range of titles. That is why roughly one out of every five books makes a profit (out of the other four, two will break even and two will lose money).

Let's pause for a moment and break this down. Publishers are producing twice as much product as they need, and have to destroy the half that doesn't sell. Of all the titles they invest time, energy, and resources into producing, only around 20% of them are making money. Naturally, this is eating into profit margins, and in today's market the eye is on the bottom line more than ever.

The logical move was to try to sell more books, but the expansion of bookselling to supermarkets and big-box stores has been a double-edged sword. While these retailers can shift huge numbers of books, this has led them to demand steep discounts from the publishers, cutting into publishers' profit margins even further. If you doubt the power these retailers hold over publishers, here is something that might change your mind: if the UK supermarket chain Tesco doesn't like a book cover, or if it clashes with their logo, it gets changed (at the publisher's expense).

As the large publishing houses search for the next big hit, some scramble to sign up top writers by offering them eye-popping advances. Once a publisher has written a big check, they have to throw some serious marketing muscle behind the book to stand any chance of recouping their outlay.

What effect has this had on the average writer? On the surface, it's not good. All those big checks leave less money for the rest. As a result, advances are falling.

Bad time to be a writer? Maybe not. After all, change brings opportunity, and in recent years, two developments have changed the industry forever: e-books and the internet.

2. Copying Mistakes Made by the Music Business

The challenges posed by digitization might be new to publishing, but they have been faced by other industries. In fact, many of the larger publishers are owned by conglomerates with significant interests in the music business.

Why did CDs eventually triumph over tapes and records? Convenience. You could skip back and forwards with ease, only selecting the tracks you wanted to hear, with no time-consuming rewinding. CDs were also small, so they didn't take up as much space as records, and the players were portable.

Digitization took all of those advantages and added low prices and even more convenience—now you only had to purchase the tracks you wanted, and you could do it from the comfort of your home. Plus, you could rip your existing CD collection and not have to fork out to replace your favorites. Once the iPod was released, the digital future was sealed.

So what about books? About a year ago I was talking with a friend about e-books. I told him the uptake was going to be far slower with e-books than it was with music because of the way people consumed books, and the emotional attachment they had to tangible printed books.

Boy, was I wrong! The swing towards e-books has been a hell of a lot faster than I, and many publishing insiders, imagined. In 2009, the American Association of Publishers (AAP) revealed that e-books made up 3% of the market. In 2010, that figure jumped above 9%. However, that yearly figure masked an explosion of sales in November that only

Delayed E-book Release

The other measure the publishing industry came up with to combat piracy—this time all on their own—was to hold back the release of an e-book version. They wanted to protect juicy hardback sales as much as possible by forcing fans to shell out for the much more expensive version first. Publishers also hoped this would allow them to make some sales before the book hit file-sharing sites.

There are several problems with this strategy. First, as mentioned above, some books are being pirated before their release dates anyway (in fact some are being pirated before there is even an e-book version; all you need is a scanner, after all). The file the publisher sends to the printers is a normal PDF file, nothing fancy. It passes through a lot of hands. It's easy to see how piracy can happen.

Second, most people who have bought e-readers don't buy physical books anymore. They feel they are paying the price for piracy by being forced to either buy an expensive print version they don't want, or wait for the e-book version. A quick trip to any Kindle users' forum will reveal this can turn a happy paying customer into an angry one who is tempted to download a pirated version.

How to Deal with Piracy

I'm going to make some suggestions on how the publishing industry can deal with piracy.

1. Stop antagonizing paying customers. This means no DRM. This means stop delaying the release of e-books. This means cut e-book prices to a reasonable level. Remove the justification from casual pirates.

2. Stop taking lessons from the music industry. One unsustainable business model seems intent on making the same mistakes of another that eviscerated itself. Good call.

3. Get those backlists online. I went looking for a Phillip K. Dick story the other day, but it's not available for the Kindle. I know there is some legal wrangling with authors over who owns the rights and what the royalty split will be, but come on, cut a deal. I also know that there are technical issues with getting backlists online, but one sure way to make piracy attractive is to not have the product on sale at all.

4. Add some value. What about some extras, like they have on DVDs? There are a million ways publishers could add value to e-books at a low cost. What about deleted scenes? Alternative endings? Historical notes? Maps? Interviews? (But don't forget to pay the author for all this extra work.)

I was tempted to add a fifth: don't sweat it. The publishing industry has already done one major thing that killed a lot of piracy before it even got started.

Think back to the music business. What led to the initial boom in illegally downloaded songs? Napster. Suddenly there was a killer app, a piece of software, that made it easy to access digital music. One of the things that made Napster so successful was that the music industry was slow to react. Simply put, there was no legal way for fans to get access to a digital version of a lot of the music they could access on Napster.

Where's the parallel here? Amazon's Kindle store. The publishing industry has a delivery method in place to reach their customers, so the chances of something like Napster-for-books coming along are slim.

Joe Konrath has repeatedly made the point on his blog that the only way to combat piracy is with convenience and price. The convenience is in place. We now have Amazon, Sony, Kobo, Barnes & Noble, Apple, and Google, as well as some individual publishers, all selling e-books, covering every possible e-reader, phone, tablet, and computer. But large publishers are still dragging their heels on price. And they have wiggle room here. As I will show in Chapter 4, over 50% of the e-book cover price is going to the publisher.

The Future

There was a lot of talk about piracy at the London Book Fair in April 2011. It was disappointing to hear one of the larger publishers insist that the e-book royalty structure was here to stay. He defended it on the premise that they couldn't raise e-book royalty rates for authors because of the increasing cost of fighting piracy. He even had the nerve to say that "unknown costs" would eat into the savings made on e-books. At least some agents pushed back on this nonsense.

This kind of talk makes me wonder if publishers are ready to cope with the challenges faced by the digital revolution or whether they are just sticking their heads in the sand.

3. Could Piracy Be Good for Authors?

When music industry revenues collapsed after the introduction of MP3s, many writers became worried. While musicians have alternative income streams, such as touring and merchandise, writers generally have just one: their words. Not even Stephen King or J.K. Rowling would fill a stadium for a reading, and most mid-list authors and new writers are lucky if there is a decent turn-out for a free bookstore event. In the last chapter I spoke about how the publishing industry's measures to combat piracy have only antagonized their paying customers, but now I want to look at piracy from a different perspective: its potential benefits. While I don't condone piracy, I do believe authors need to challenge their assumptions about this issue.

Piracy: a Tax on Success

First off, piracy can almost be viewed as a tax on success. Writers who are only selling a handful of copies a month don't tend to be pirated. Why would the hackers bother? It's the authors of popular books—those appearing in the bestseller lists—who are targeted.

Mark Coker, the founder of Smashwords, insists that all work sold on his site is DRM-free. To Coker's mind, the greatest threat a writer faces is not piracy—it's obscurity. Anything that makes work less accessible and less enjoyable makes it more obscure.

Coker identifies two kinds of pirates: the "scoundrels and cheapskates who will never pay for anything... [and] don't represent a lost sale," and those who feel justified in pirating work because it's only available in certain formats, it's priced too high, or it's not for sale in their territory. This second group does represent *some* lost sales.

Nothing can be done about the first group, but writers need to think about how to tackle the second. Mark Coker points out that "piracy is an indication that your work is in demand"—a demand that is only being filled by pirates because you have failed to make purchasing preferable to pirating.

The way to combat piracy is with convenience and price. Your work should be available in all formats, so it can be read on any e-reader, and on sale with as many retailers as possible, DRM-free, without territory restrictions, and priced fairly so customers have less incentive to steal it.

Neil Gaiman, Joe Konrath and Piracy

Internationally best-selling author Neil Gaiman used to be dead against piracy, but his views have evolved since he noticed two things. In countries where his work was being pirated, his sales went up. He convinced his publisher to let him put his novel *American Gods*, which was still selling well, up on his website for anyone to download and share. Sales of all of his books increased 300%.

Gaiman also argues that authors are not losing sales through piracy. At the end of each of his readings he asks the audience how they discovered their favorite writers. He estimates only 5% to 10% actually purchased the book, the rest were lent the book by a friend or received it as a gift. He now concludes that piracy is "people lending books" and amounts to free advertising.

Joe Konrath has similar views but understands why many writers fear piracy. To test his theories, Konrath decided to conduct an experiment. He gave a free book away on his website—the same book that was on sale on Amazon for $1.99—and encouraged pirates to download it in a blog post called "Steal This E-book." He then asked them to push it out to all of the file-sharing sites. Not only did his sales increase overall, his sales increased for that book too—even though he raised the sale price of the Amazon edition by a dollar halfway through!

Meanwhile, the publishing industry seems blind to any other perspective on piracy. Most larger houses insist on putting DRM on e-books, restricting territories, and holding back the release of e-books to protect print sales. In addition to this, they have been pushing for legislation to allow them to sue their customers.

Why are they so insistent on making the same mistakes as the music industry?

4. Royalties

People often ask how much money a writer makes per copy sold. The short answer is, not much (and as you will see below, it's the wrong question). I think it would be useful to show how the money you hand over for your books is divvied up. There are exceptions to the foregoing, but it holds true in the case of most large publishers.

A $25 Hardback

Retailer: 50% ($12.50)
Publisher: 37.5% ($9.38)
Writer: 12.5% ($3.12 minus an agent's 15% cut, leaving $2.66)

Don't forget, the retailer has to pay staff, overheads, advertising, and storage. The publisher has all of that, plus production costs.

An $8 Mass-market Paperback

Retailer: 50% ($4)
Publisher: 40% ($3.20)
Writer: 10% ($0.80, minus agent's 15% cut, leaving $0.68)

A paperback represents a lower author take per copy, but an author expects to shift a hell of a lot more in paperback than in hardback.

A $9.99 Trade-published E-book

Retailer: 30% ($2.99)
Publisher: 52.5% ($5.25)
Writer: 17.5% ($1.75, minus agent's 15% cut, leaving $1.49)

Most publishers like to say they pay a royalty rate of 25% to their authors. However, this is before the retailer's cut is deducted (and the agent fees, if an author has an agent). Thus, the "net" sum an author receives (before they pay tax on their earnings) may be as low as 14.9% if they have an agent. The retailer keeps 30% of the cost of the book and hands 70% to the publisher. The publisher then gives 25% of *that* to the writer, which is 17.5% of the cover price. The agent takes 15% of that, leaving the writer with 14.9% of the cover price.

An e-book retailer has fewer overheads (no storage or shipping costs) so the publisher forces a lower cut on them, but the publisher has fewer overheads too (and no print costs), yet they are still holding on to a stunning 52.5%.

It doesn't take a genius to figure out why publishers are keen to hold back the digital tide—they make nearly twice as much off a hardback as they do off an e-book (despite the higher percentages). However, publishers' e-book pricing policy has also been controversial. Publishing houses want to keep the price of e-books high in order to protect the sales of physical books. Most e-book releases from traditional publishers are priced between $7.99 and $12.99.

Small independent presses can be more flexible with their pricing (and pay higher royalty rates) because they have much lower overheads. Self-publishers have even fewer overheads, and many are prepared to sell at the lowest possible price ($0.99) or to give their work away for free in order to entice readers.

Large publishers, therefore, face further problems. When retailers such as Amazon discount print books, it can leave the e-book version more expensive than the hardback. Readers, of course, cannot understand why an e-book should cost more than a printed book, and many have been showing their displeasure by giving one-star reviews to such releases on Amazon, and organizing boycotts.

A $2.99 Self-published E-book

Retailer: 30% ($0.90)
Writer: 70% ($2.09, and usually no agent to get a cut)

Authors who publish their own e-books, without the help of publishing houses or agents, get a bigger piece of the pie. With Amazon (and the other retailers are similar), the author keeps 70% of the sale price if the e-book is priced between $2.99 and $9.99. If they price it below $2.99 or above $9.99 they keep 35% (although the latter rarely happens, for obvious reasons).

Either way, that's considerably more than 14.9%, whichever way you slice it. *Part Two* examines pricing strategies for selling e-books, but it might be useful to run some numbers now to contrast trade publisher and self-publisher royalty rates.

An author with a trade-published e-book receives 14.9% in royalties (after an agent's deductions). For a $9.99 e-book, that's $1.49 a copy. If they sell 5,000 copies, this leaves them with $7,450.

A self-publisher with an e-book priced at $2.99 is getting $2.09 per copy. This means they only need to sell 3,565 copies to make the same money, and at less than one-third of the cover price! Of course, many independent authors are selling a lot more than that, and some at higher prices too.

If a self-published author prices work at $3.99, he or she will get around $2.79 a copy, meaning they'll only need to sell 2,670 copies to beat the trade deal. At $4.99, the author's cut jumps to $3.49, meaning they only need to sell 2,134 copies to make the same amount of cash.

Advances

The unfortunate truth is that most traditionally published authors (with the larger houses) never see any royalties. To understand why, we need to talk a little about advances. When a writer sells a book to a publishing house (with or without an agent's assistance), they receive an advance on future royalties. The advance offered varies and depends on a huge number of variables, but for a debut novel the average writer receives around $5,000. This average includes small publishing houses and New York publishers, but even if you are just talking about the Big Six publishers, unless you're lucky enough to be involved in a "bidding war," the average only rises to approximately $10,000. A writer with a few novels under his or her belt (and subsequent sales), may be looking at advances of up to $20,000 with the Big Six.

Obviously, the more copies an author sells of his or her first book, the more competition there will be for the second, pushing the advance higher. Industry estimates suggest that out of every five books, one makes a profit, two break even, and two lose money. Only 20% of books earn out their advance.

The writer also doesn't get all of the advance money up front. Typically, the advance is spread out over three payments: one on signing the publishing contract, another on acceptance of the final version of the manuscript, and another on publication (although thriller writer James Rollins said his last advance was split into *five* payments, with the last two being made on publication of the paperback and one year later). As the publication process usually takes 12 to 18 months or longer, the writer must wait quite a while before they see the fruits of their labor.

Most books don't earn out. In other words, they don't sell enough copies to cover the amount of royalties the publisher would have paid out without an advance. It's important to point out that this doesn't mean the publisher has lost money on those books, just that they made less than they estimated they would.

Because of the returns policy, a book doesn't have much time to convince a publisher it could be the one out of five that will make them money. Some booksellers start returning books after one month if it appears they have ordered too many. This means that advance check (or three checks) is all the money most authors are going to see for that book. Ever.

However, when an author self-publishes a book online there is no pressure to remove it from sale because there is an infinite amount of virtual shelf space. There is no reason why an author can't have his or her entire backlist on sale all the time, making money.

All of the production costs are at the start, and, as I'll cover later, can be kept to a minimum. Everything after that is profit. You don't get an advance, but what's a one-off payment versus getting paid forever?

5. What We Talk About When We Talk About Editing

A lot of the focus on my blog, in the news, and in this book has been on the challenges the digital revolution poses for trade publishing houses. Most of the talk is about what is best for writers, and how they will be affected. Now I want to talk about editors.

Editors are the unsung heroes of the publishing world. While some editors might have made a name for themselves within the industry, they mostly remain anonymous to the reader. Yet the books that readers buy would not be the same without them. Editors have suffered the most from the upheaval in the publishing industry, and I fear their pain will worsen as the Big Six continue to make missteps.

Commissioning editors acquire books from agents and authors, although their power to do so has diminished in recent times and they almost always need approval from sales and marketing before they can make an offer. But, aside from that, what do editors do?

Well, they edit. They take an author's work and turn it into the story the writer meant to put down on the page. They have the requisite emotional distance from the work to cut without remorse, tighten prose, and make writing more powerful. They comb the story for plot holes, red herrings, clichés, cardboard characters, split infinitives, and dangling participles. They cross-reference, they fact-check, and they nudge flabby prose back into line. Some writers need more work on their manuscripts than others, but all writers need editors.

Take Raymond Carver, a legendary short story writer and

master of economy. You would struggle to find a wasted word in much of his work. His long-time editor, Gordon Lish, worked with some of the biggest names: Ken Kesey, Neil Cassady, Allen Ginsberg, Jack Kerouac, Don DeLillo and T.C. Boyle, as well as Nabakov and Kundera.

Carver's prose wouldn't have been the same without Lish's input. If you want to see that for yourself, *The New Yorker* published the original draft of Carver's famous story "What We Talk About When We Talk About Love," with his editor's corrections visible. I recommend you read it in full (nyr.kr/lishcarver); when you do, you will see Lish's contribution is huge. He even came up with the title (it was originally called "Beginners"—not quite as catchy).

Gordon Lish was no one-off. There are excellent editors who improve every book they work on in every imprint of every trade publishing house. Some of them, like Gordon Lish, are fine writers in their own right. But they are under threat. Consolidation of several big players in the industry led to downsizing, and many talented editors were let go. Some ended up at other houses; others founded their own small presses or became agents. Many, however, were lost to the business. With the inevitable next round of lay-offs, we may lose even more. But it's not all doom and gloom. I think the digital revolution will eventually lead to an increase in readership, with people now reading on computers, laptops, tablets, e-readers and smartphones—some of them people who haven't bought a book in years. Readers will always want new books, and writers will always need editors.

While some self-publishers have decided to take their books to market without using an editor, this always shows, and readers are great at separating the wheat from the chaff.

Writers shouldn't consider editing an expense; they should consider it an investment. The smart ones already do. There will be more and more freelance work in this brave new world. There will be opportunities to partner with agents and set up new companies that help writers with design, editing, formatting, and marketing. And maybe, without having to deal with all that corporate crap, editors will have a chance to spend more time doing what they really enjoy: editing. They will be able to work on challenging fiction without having to get the nod from sales and marketing, and they will be able to help a writer grow, without worrying that poor sales figures on debut novels will see their authors cut loose.

A good editor can be one of the clear advantages of going with a trade publisher rather than self-publishing, so what is an indie writer to do? Later, in *Part Two*, I will talk about your options.

6. Literary Agents

In our mad dash around the new publishing landscape, there's one group we have only mentioned in passing: literary agents. Nothing in the publishing world inspires more diverse reactions than the mention of agents.

For some they are the holy grail, the star-makers, the gatekeepers to the dream factory. Others are less kind, and I won't repeat their opinions. Suffice to say some writers view agents as amoral Svengalis and an additional, superfluous barrier between writers and publishers (and readers).

The truth is somewhere in between. Agents, as with any profession, run the full gamut of experience, ability, competency, and propriety. Some can send a writer's career into the stratosphere; others may actually prove detrimental.

For those unfamiliar with an agent's role, agents are authors' representatives. Their primary role is to sell books to editors and negotiate deals on the author's behalf, and they also seek to monetize the author's work in other ways by selling foreign language rights, audiobook rights, movie rights, and so on.

For this, they take a cut of the author's royalties, usually 15%. But because they don't take any money up-front for their services (at least, scrupulous ones don't), an agent will only take on an author they think might make them money.

Ok, so that's the basics covered. What I want to ask is what happens to agents in a future where most people are reading e-books? After all, you don't need an agent to self-publish, and fewer authors are likely to seek a trade publishing deal when all the money is in digital and the royalty rates are up to four times higher going it alone.

If agents have no books to sell to editors, they have 15% of nothing. So how are they planning for tomorrow? Different agents have responded to this question in different ways, leading to an obvious rift in the publishing community.

Agents Becoming Publishers

In May 2011, *The Bookseller* reported that Ed Victor, one of the top UK agents, had announced he was setting up his own publishing division—Bedford Square Books.

Andrew Wylie made waves last year when he announced Odyssey Editions—his own imprint to publish his authors' backlists (including Roth, Bellow, and Updike), the rights of which had reverted from trade deals. Scott Waxman has also set up his own publishing company, called Diversion Books.

However, some powerhouse agencies, such as Trident, insist, "it is a mistake for agents to become publishers. There are substantial conflicts of interests involved." In the UK, Sonia Land walked away from a publishing deal to go it alone with e-versions of Catherine Cookson's estate. Piers Blofeld, of the same agency, has called for a change in the code of conduct governing UK agents (it currently precludes publishers as members). Other top agents, like Simon Trewin, have cautioned against this.

Ed Victor's move is particularly newsworthy because he was the first well-known UK agent to announce that, on top of publishing backlists as e-books, he will be seeking the stars of tomorrow. He is offering a 50/50 split with his authors on e-royalties. This sounds okay, but when you examine it closely, it all falls apart.

The first problem is that the split is after the retailer gets their 30% of the list price. It is also after the producer of the book—a digital production company called Acorn Independent Publishing—gets a percentage too.

The Bookseller article also says that net receipts won't be

divvied up until "production costs" are covered, but doesn't say if these are referring to the percentage going to Acorn, or further costs such as marketing and promotion.

Ed Victor may have the best of intentions, but there are a few reasons why I think this is a terrible deal for writers. First off, it's absolutely crazy to be paying a digital production company a percentage of your royalties forever instead of a flat fee. There are plenty of companies out there who do top-quality work for a fee—no need to pay a percentage.

Also, the author ends up with a lot less than 50%. Once Amazon gets its cut (30%), and Acorn get their cut (for the sake of argument, let's say 10%), that leaves the writer and Ed Victor to split 60%—leaving 30% each.

Finally, if these "production costs" are not coming out of Ed Victor's percentage (the article seems to indicate this is not the case) and are not accounted for in Acorn's percentage (the article is unclear), then the writer gets even less than 30%.

This is not significantly better than a trade publishing house, is far worse than what an author would get in some smaller presses, and is less than half what they would get from self-publishing.

Plus, the best agent in the world might know a lot about contracts and royalty statements and how to sell books to trade houses, as well as how to sell foreign rights and movie rights, but they might know nothing about how to produce a successful book and get it into the hands of lots of readers.

How much does the average literary agent understand about Amazon rankings, Google PageRank, Twitter, Facebook Pages, Goodreads, SEO, cover design, formatting, editing, CPC, CPM, regional targeting, AdWords, blogging, spam laws, Shelfari, or blurb copywriting?

How much do they know about tagging, proofing, pricing strategies, DRM, giveaways, digital piracy, EPUB, Kobo, link tracking, mailing lists, MOBI, effective back-matter, Smashwords, KDP, or PubIt?

These are just some of the many things a digital publisher will have to get their head around. And, looking at the production levels, the covers, the formatting, the front matter, and the Amazon rankings of some of the Catherine Cookson e-books, I would respectfully suggest that these skills have yet to be mastered.

Right now an author has four choices with a manuscript: a major publisher, a smaller press, self-publishing, or one of these new agent–publisher hybrids. My advice to anyone weighing their options is to think very carefully before going with an agent–publisher. The royalty rates are bad and they don't have experience in breaking new digital authors.

Some may turn out to be good at it—I'm sure some will—but I wouldn't want to be the lab rat. None of the agent–publishers, as far as I am aware, have broken a new digital star, even though some of their operations have been going for more than a year.

Plenty of large trade houses have done it. Plenty of small presses have done it. Plenty of self-publishers have done it. Consider those three options first. Choose according to your circumstances.

If you don't want to deal with the minutiae of self-publishing, there are plenty of companies that provide a one-stop shop such as Ed Victor is proposing, but they only charge a flat fee. Telemachus Press is one. John Locke uses them and he is doing just fine.

There's only one thing in *The Bookseller* article that made sense to me. Ed Victor said that, in this turbulent future, what he brings to the table is an ability to be "lighter on his feet." That's true: there are advantages to being smaller and nimbler in changing times.

But you can't get smaller and nimbler than a self-publisher. If you don't want to go that way, I would take the experience, marketing power, and advance of a trade publisher over an agent–publisher hybrid anytime.

Also, there is one final problem with Ed Victor's venture. An agent is supposed to be the author's advocate, and the publisher's interest isn't always aligned with the writer's. Blurring those lines makes it difficult to be an independent advocate. There are conflict of interest issues here. If your agent becomes a publisher, how do you know she will seek the best deal for you when publishing your work herself is the best deal for her?

In fairness to agents, some have come out strongly against this nonsense. Trident in the US and Peter Cox in the UK have been particularly vocal about why this is such a bad idea. But many others are considering joining the fray, such as Curtis Brown (UK).

We will see a lot more of this in the future. Writers need to be on their guard. Don't give away a percentage of your future earnings unless it's for a trade deal you can't say no to.

As for agents, there is another way for them to make money in this brave new world, and agencies like Trident are leading the way, but we will get to that in Chapter 12.

7. The 800lb Gorilla: Amazon

In trying to create a snapshot of the rapidly changing publishing landscape, we have taken a look at the challenges facing traditional houses, the rising digital tide, how the price of a book breaks down, piracy, and agents moving into publishing. Now we are going to talk about the 800-Pound Gorilla.

Amazon opened its doors in 1995 and has been making headlines ever since, aggressively pursuing market share over profits. Less than two years after they started trading they were sued by Barnes & Noble for claiming to be the world's largest bookstore. The matter was settled out of court (and Amazon continued to use the slogan). Nobody would challenge that claim now.

The company expanded quickly, opening four European sites, one in Canada, and one each in Japan and China, in the process changing the shopping habits of customers worldwide.

Today, Amazon sells a range of products and services, and, more importantly for the purposes of this book, they currently control around 60% of the US e-book market and are on the way to controlling 50% of the *overall* US book market by the end of 2012.

In addition, Amazon partners with specialist, independent, and used bookstores, provides the most popular digital self-publishing platform, and has expanded into Print-on-Demand, audiobooks, and social-networking. If that isn't enough, they also manufacture the top-selling dedicated e-reader, the Kindle.

The Kindle

E-readers have been knocking around, in one form or another, since the late 1990s, but didn't really take off until Amazon got into the game.

The very first Kindle was released in November 2007, retailing at $399. It sold out in five-and-a-half hours, remaining out of stock until late April 2008. In the face of competition from Barnes & Noble, Sony, Kobo, and Apple, successive versions were released with greater memory capacity, expanded functionality, wireless capability, rudimentary browsers, and greatly reduced price. The market exploded.

In January 2011, the Kindle 3, on sale for just four months, overtook the final book in the Harry Potter series to become the top-selling item in Amazon's history. While the company has remained tight-lipped on exactly how many Kindles it has shipped since day one, industry estimates place this figure at 15 million, with a market share of 59%—and that was before the release of the lower-priced, ad-supported Kindle.

To highlight the challenge facing bricks-and-mortar booksellers, Amazon was estimated to have sold 4 million e-books on Christmas Day alone.

Kindle Direct Publishing

In 2007, Amazon launched their own digital publishing platform, allowing anybody who owned the rights to a book to upload an electronic version for sale to the general public. The rights-holder (i.e. the publisher or author) could set the price they chose and receive 35% commission, with Amazon keeping the rest.

But it wasn't until 2009, when the Kindle started to sell in real numbers, that successful print authors, such as Joe

Konrath, started to experiment with selling e-books. Konrath enjoyed a solid, if unspectacular, mid-list career before he decided to e-publish some of his books that had been rejected by his publishers—books he had been giving away free on his website. While he wasn't the first to publish e-books with Amazon, he was the first to share his sales figures. Straight away he was making $1,000 a month.

Sony, Barnes & Noble, Kobo, and Apple soon all began offering digital platforms for authors to sell their work. For the first time, self-publishers had access to a distribution network that could rival anything trade publishing could access. Additionally, the low cost of publishing an e-book meant many writers could consider self-publishing for the first time.

Trade-published writers whose backlist titles had fallen out of print also began publishing them as e-books. Unpublished writers, unable to crack trade publishing, began publishing themselves. By the end of 2010, Konrath had forsaken traditional publishing, released a string of self-published titles, and was selling 1,000 copies a day. He had also become an evangelist for self-publishing, and his sales figures represented a thorn in the side of traditional publishing.

Previously unpublished writers were raking it in too. Amanda Hocking, unable to convince an agent to take her on, sold a million e-books in nine months! Then John Locke, who never even sent a query letter to an agent, became the first indie writer to hold the top spot in the Amazon Kindle 100, selling a staggering 350,000 copies in the first two months of 2011 and around the same number again in March alone. By June, he was announced as the eighth author, and the first self-publisher, to sell a million Kindle books—most of those in five months.

The Agency Agreement

Amazon was approaching a virtual monopoly of the e-book market at the beginning of 2010, and the larger publishers knew they had to do something. If a business sells all of their widgets to one customer, that customer controls their pricing policy. Publishers could not allow Amazon to continue heavily discounting e-books. They needed to allow other players to gain some foothold in the market to prevent Amazon from abusing its dominant position.

The Big Six publishers proposed the Agency Agreement (also known as the Agency Model), which stated that e-book prices would be set by the publisher, not the retailer, and that no discounting would be allowed. It also set the 70/30 split in which retailers kept 30% of the cover price of the e-book and the rest went to the publisher to divvy out as they saw fit.

Amazon fought hard against the agreement, going as far as to remove Macmillan's books from sale. The publishers were backed by the agents and, with Apple cozying up to the publishers, Amazon was forced to back down and sign the Agency Agreement.

The Future

When Amazon could no longer price new entrants out of the market, its competitors' sales boomed. Now, the marketplace has leveled out a little. The rest of the world remains far behind the US in terms of e-book market share and e-reader sales, but some trends are developing. Apple is emerging as a key competitor in Europe. Kobo has been making inroads in Australia. Gradually, Amazon is losing market share to hungry competitors.

The 60% or so US e-book market share I mentioned at the start of this chapter sounds impressive, but that has dropped from a high of near 90%. Barnes & Noble is grabbing between 20% and 25%, while Kobo, Sony, Apple, and Google share out 15% to 20%.

But while Amazon's share of the e-book market is diminishing, the overall market is growing—rapidly. Amazon can be confident of future profits. Self-publishers and trade-published authors with reverted rights on backlist titles are in pretty good shape too. Since the Agency Agreement they earn double the royalty rate, keeping 70% of their books' cover price at certain price points.

At the start of 2011, Amazon VP Russ Grandinetti declared that, "however fast you think this change is happening, it's probably happening faster than you think."

It's probably happening faster than anyone thinks, except for Joe Konrath. He's now making $50,000 a month.

8. Print Is Doomed

While I might beat the self-publishing drum at times, I don't celebrate when I hear publishers are in trouble or bookstores are closing down, because there are people behind the headlines. Foreclosures and lay-offs have ramifications for the entire book industry and the closure of bookstores, in particular, is disheartening.

When people say—as a lot of my friends do—that they have no interest in e-books and can't imagine ever using an e-reader, I get it. People have an emotional attachment to print books. You see them wandering the aisles of bookstores, stroking books' spines as if they were long lost lovers. Some take a book from the shelf, open it carefully, close their eyes, and inhale. They trace their fingers beneath words. They caress pages.

Books are beautiful things. I have a strong attachment to them myself. I don't want a future without bookstores and where printed books are a rarity. Unfortunately, I have very little say in what the future is actually going to be like.

It may come as a shock to some, but I don't own an e-reader. In fact, I only bought my first e-book in April 2011. I read e-books on my laptop, but I find that having the internet a click away makes it difficult to immerse myself in what I'm reading for a sustained length of time. I bought the book in digital form only because there was no print version.

I think this will become more common. It's much cheaper to produce digital-only versions. While some costs remain the same (cover design, editing, marketing), a whole bunch of other costs (storage, printing, returns) don't even exist in the digital world. That alone makes e-books less of a financial risk. Publishers, especially small publishers and self-publishers, are now producing a lot of editions exclusively as e-books. But there is another threat to print books and those who publish them.

Bookstores are in trouble. Borders, the second-largest chain in the US, has filed for Chapter 11 Bankruptcy Protection and may end up being liquidated. The largest, Barnes & Noble, has planned a huge amount of store closures, are seeking a buyer, and are only showing growth in their online operations.

In Australia, the book industry was shocked by the sudden collapse of REDgroup Retail, the parent group for bookstores Borders and Angus & Robertson, two of Australia's largest book retailers. Waterstone's is closing hundreds of stores across the UK and only found a buyer after being on the market for some time. The largest chain in Ireland is under pressure and has undergone another round of restructuring and re-branding. The second largest went out of business last year.

When a chain goes down, it doesn't just affect the shareholders and the workers, it has repercussions throughout the industry. Towns are often left without a bookstore, forcing people online. Publishers are left with fewer outlets to distribute to, and lower orders, which hurts distributors and writers.

Some feel that struggling chains deserve what they are getting and that their increasingly homogenous selections and demands for greater discounts from publishers have left them with few friends in the publishing world.

If this is your view, ask yourself one question: what do you think it will be like when the only physical place you can buy a book is at a supermarket?

While large chains stocked limited selections in some respects and may have made it difficult for self-publishers and smaller presses to get their books stocked, it is far worse in Tesco and Walmart, which stock only a tiny selection and tend to go for safer bets.

Independent bookstores, on the other hand, have smaller margins and less cash reserves, and rarely attract outside investment. Often they are a labor of love and their owners appear more willing to take risks on new writers or on unusual books, rather than making decisions strictly on a profit or loss basis.

Like smaller presses, indie bookstores will nurture a writer and may give a book time to find an audience, rather than returning it to the publisher after a month. They talk to customers, to find out what they like, and may ask them to consider something a little different.

They host readings, poetry nights, and book clubs, all of which rarely make them money but help build a community around the store. Owners of indie bookstores are book-lovers themselves, and their passion shines through.

The downside to this is that their books tend to be more expensive. In the past, customers of independent bookstores were willing to pay more in return for a diverse selection and a personal touch. However Amazon, with virtually any book a couple of clicks away, has stolen a lot of their business.

As a result, a string of venerable indie bookstores—real institutions—closed their doors in 2010. Many more have announced they need either investors or a buyer to avoid going the same way.

Digital guru Mike Shatzkin suggests that if bookstores lose another 15% of their trade they will go out of business. Sales figures for February showed print books were down 34.4% year-on-year. The numbers bounced back in March but collapsed again the following month. The future looks bleak.

If this keeps up, pretty soon the only place you will be able to buy a print book will be in a supermarket or online. If you don't like e-books, and you can't see yourself using an e-reader, there is something you can do about it: go to your local bookstore and buy a book. But do it while you can, because the way things are going, they may not be around for much longer.

9. E-book Dominance Is Inevitable

I have a confession to make: I've never really liked hardbacks. Now, don't get me wrong, I like looking at them. I like touching them. I like holding them. I think they are beautiful *objects*. I just don't like reading them. They are cumbersome, heavy, uncomfortable to read when lying down, and difficult to lug from place to place.

They are also expensive. The cloth cover, acid-free paper, and pristine dust jacket all cost money. In setting the recommended retail price, the publisher factors in storage, delivery, and returns, as well as free review and promotional copies, so there are a lot of costs to pass on to the reader.

But it's not all bad for the publishers. They love hardbacks for a reason—there's a healthy margin. Authors love them too. And distributors. And booksellers. Hardbacks are far juicier all round than trade paperbacks (the outsize paperback that is becoming more common) or mass-market paperbacks (the common, smaller, cheaper paperback). Because publishers, distributors, and booksellers all have an interest in protecting hardback sales, other formats are sometimes held back to maximize hardback revenue.

Problem is, people aren't buying it anymore. Hardback sales have collapsed. Let's take a look at historic adult trade sales from the American Association of Publishers (AAP) for the month of February. In 2007, adult hardback sales were $111.9 million for February. For the next three years they dropped to around $80 million. In February 2011, they plummeted to $46.2 million.

There is little doubt that e-publishing and the increased popularity of self-publishing are squeezing hardback sales, but it is not all about money. Trade paperbacks are cheaper than hardbacks, but even they are down from a high of $128.8 million in 2006 to $81.2 million in 2011. Mass-market paperbacks are cheaper again, often priced at just $7 or $8 a book, but sales of them have also dropped from $59.5 million in 2008 to only $29.3 million in 2011.

E-book pessimists, who concede the hardback is in trouble and will continue to lose market share, seem to think paperbacks will buck this trend and that e-books will plateau soon.

I'm not sure there is much evidence for that. The internet has revolutionized every industry it has come into contact with; publishing is no different. The pace at which e-books sales are growing comes as a surprise only to those who forget how instrumental this technology has been in changing other industries.

The book industry isn't very good at collating accurate, up-to-date figures, and doesn't often share all the information collected. Amazon is particularly tight-lipped. As publishing moves towards a future in which most print sales will be made online and the majority of book sales will be e-books, this should give some cause for concern.

We can only work with the figures we have, and, even if they don't reflect the entire market, the underlying trends are obvious. The AAP regularly collects data from trade publishers and breaks it down to provide information on various formats: e-books, audiobooks, and print (which, in turn, is subdivided into children's and adults' hardback, mass-market paperback, and trade paperback).

While their statistics only cover their members, 84 houses report print data and 16 report e-book data to give a snapshot of the industry. The standard measure of how well e-books are selling is to express their sales as a percentage of the entire trade print market (all those sub-divisions I mentioned above) plus e-books.

Here are some historical figures from the AAP showing

the market share of all trade books that e-books have captured:

2005: 0.3%
2006: 0.5%
2007: 0.6%
2008: 1.2%
2009: 3.2%
2010: 8.3%

That's some pretty spectacular growth. But what those figures don't show is an explosion in the popularity of e-books in November 2010—a surge that carried right through until February 2011, when e-books became the #1 selling format for the first time, capturing 29.5% of the market (more than hardback *and* more than paperback).

Bear in mind that this figure only includes trade publishers; it doesn't include most smaller presses, e-publishers, and self-publishers. Once those are added to the mix, e-books could have been more than one-third of all book sales in February 2011!

In the next two sets of figures the AAP released (they are usually around two months after the fact), e-books slipped back to third position, but the overall trend is clear. E-books are surging, and for the first four months of 2011 they had grown more than 150% to capture around 20% of the market.

Why did e-books slip back? Well, many products are seasonal for one reason or another. For print books, the period in the run-up to Christmas is the busiest time of year.

Naturally, whenever there is a peak, there is also a trough. Summer months make up the trough for e-book sales, which makes sense because people are more likely to be outdoors rather than inside reading. It remains to be seen whether this trend will continue because, when the market is this young, figures will be skewed by newcomers attracted by new models of e-readers at increasingly lower prices.

Many experts have tried to dampen down some of the speculation over how much of the market e-books could capture. Some suggest there is a natural high-water mark that e-books can't go beyond and have pegged this at 50% or less. I'm not so sure.

Boomers Driving Adoption

Early adopters tend to be an indicator of where a market is going, but an interesting thing about e-books is that a lot of change is being driven by the older generation, as a Pew Research Center study in February 2011 titled "Generations & Gadgets" confirmed.

Frustrated with the smaller selection, limited availability, and extra cost (and weight) of large print books, baby boomers have been turning to e-readers in droves, delighted with the ability to resize the font at will.

Those with eyesight difficulties have also been early adopters. But these aren't the only factors driving change.

Feedback Loops

Tim Spalding of LibraryThing contends that "the logic of e-books' success has inbuilt feedback loops." In other words, at a certain point success becomes self-perpetuating.

In an extremely prescient article published in November 2010, he gave his reasoning. As e-books increase in popularity, they will cannibalize print sales, forcing booksellers out of business. This will make print books harder to find, less convenient, and less popular—increasing the popularity of e-books.

As the number of bookstores decreases, print runs are reduced—forcing up costs, and thus retail prices. At the same time, e-books are getting cheaper. The cost in producing e-books is fixed—there are no marginal costs—and as volume increases, that cost gets spread out even more. As print becomes more and more expensive to produce (pushing up prices), e-books will just get cheaper to publish.

He further contends that simple economics will lead to a greater selection of titles available in digital-only formats, making e-readers a necessity, which will itself drive e-books sales, continuing the feedback loop. The point, in brief, is that all of the factors that are now driving e-book success will amplify, leading to a virtuous circle of growth while print is caught in a vicious circle of decline.

Spalding's article was written when e-books made up just 7% of the market. He prefaced his argument by saying that when e-books rose far above 20% of the market and became the dominant book format, these feedback loops would come into play.

We are there already. Print is in freefall. Bookstores are closing down. Print is becoming a subsidiary right. And we aren't even close to saturation point yet. A lot more people will buy dedicated e-readers this year. Even more people will buy tablets of some sort. Many more again will buy new smartphones.

More and more consumers are going to come into contact with e-books for the first time. When they do—when they discover the advantages: the convenience, the instant availability, the portability, the increasing selection, the reduced cost per title—many are going to switch from print. It doesn't matter if a sizable portion of readers still prefer print; the printed book's lack of viability will threaten those who publish it, distribute it, and sell it, ultimately restricting the selection of those who read it.

Just as success becomes self-perpetuating, so does failure. Borders' future will be decided shortly; whatever emerges (if anything) it will not be the bookselling force of the past.

Barnes & Noble is showing growth only online and in

non-book products. More and more bookshelves are being replaced with Nook display areas, toys, and games. Less shelf space means more books by mid-list authors in the warehouse, or never ordered to begin with. This leads to lower print runs, which increases printing costs, which increases book prices, which sends more people online seeking discounts or encourages them to switch to e-books, which leads to lower bookstore sales of books, which leads to... you get the idea.

If you want to see where the future is headed, look at Amazon. In May 2011, they announced they were selling more e-books than all print categories combined.

This is a death spiral for print, and it's not going to be pretty. At some point, print fans may be forced to choose between extremely expensive limited edition hardbacks and going digital. As e-readers, tablets and smartphones become more sophisticated—and cheaper—the e-book revolution will spread beyond the borders of America and go global.

10. Publishers: The New Travel Agents?

Previous chapters examined various aspects of the publishing industry, assessing how different parts are faring in the face of the changes brought about by the internet and e-publishing.

As any travel agent will tell you (if you can find one), the internet is an unstoppable force that transforms any business it comes into contact with. In publishing, change initially seemed sluggish. However, below the surface, the internet has been quietly eroding the very foundations of publishing.

Online Shopping

The first big change was the advent of online shopping. Amazon revolutionized the way people buy books. Consumers might have missed the personal touch offered by their local bookstore, but for most this was trumped by much cheaper prices, an enormous selection that could be browsed online from anywhere, and the added convenience of having them delivered direct to the door (in some cases for free).

Obviously, this sales model took business from booksellers, but it has also chipped away at the notion of "curated selection"—the idea that someone else can decide what books a reader buys. If it's in print, then Amazon sells it. If it's not, then they probably have a used copy.

The term "gatekeepers" in publishing usually refers to agents and editors dictating which books get published and which don't. But there are actually plenty more gatekeepers than that; a book must be "sold" several times before it gets to a reader.

Marketing teams and salespeople decide which titles to push hard to booksellers. Publishers vie for maximum exposure in stores, but only for certain books. Even whether the book is "spine out" or "face out" is for sale, and publishers decide which books get what kind of backing. The number one "gatekeeper," of course, is the bookseller, who decides which titles to stock and in what numbers.

All of these gatekeepers have less power to curate when readers are bypassing bookstores in favor of the convenience, price, and near-infinite selection of Amazon. When everything is available online, the power of vetting and curation passes to the readers.

Freedom of Information

The linking up of computers across the world, tied to the ability of people to share information instantly and make it universally accessible and searchable, has changed the way everyone does business.

It has enabled booksellers to access up-to-the-minute sales data in all their stores, publishers to obtain a reasonably accurate picture of how their titles are doing at any given time, and writers to get an idea of how their book might perform before it even goes on sale.

However, this has intensified the problems publishers face with the "sale or return" model. More than ever, a book is under pressure to perform in its first few weeks on sale. Titles are rarely given an opportunity to build an audience.

Booksellers know straight away which books are selling and which aren't, and can return the under-performers before they have a chance to find an audience.

E-books

In April 2011, Amazon announced that they were selling more e-books than print books. Trade publishers played down these figures, (correctly) pointing out that this included a lot of cheaply priced titles.

However, this misses the point. E-books are outselling print books! The cost of producing e-books is much lower, so it makes sense to charge less for them. And, publishers have much higher margins on e-books. The only reason publishers are pricing them so high is to both shore up print sales and to check Amazon's growth.

Plus, this matters little to self-publishers, who make more royalties from a $2.99 sale than they would through a publisher at $9.99.

E-mail Submissions

Any agent or editor will tell you the decision to accept e-mail submissions has hugely affected the number they receive. Before, writers had to go to the trouble and expense of printing their manuscripts out, buying envelopes and stamps, hunting down the address of the agency or publisher, and then mailing their work (along with an SAE), and waiting.

Now, using e-mail an author can send a manuscript to every agent and editor in the country for free. Agents and publishers expend significant resources and manpower just to deal with the fire-hose of submissions.

Usually, the first reader is an intern, who may or may not have the skill or judgment to assess a submission accurately. This isn't a complaint; it's a fact. Most agencies or publishing companies simply cannot afford to have full-time, qualified, experienced agents or editors reading all submissions; if they did, they would go out of business. A side-effect of that is many fine writers get lost in the slushpile. Until recently, these authors had little viable choice but to press on, keep submitting and keep hoping.

Digital Self-publishing

Now, all authors have another choice: self-publishing. Of course, self-publishing has always existed, but it only became a realistic option for most writers with the boom in e-readers. Before the advent of e-books, the cost of self-publishing a printed edition was prohibitive for most authors, and distribution was a real problem: bookstores weren't interested.

Cue the e-book and, for the first time, writers who couldn't crack traditional publishing could publish themselves and match the distributive power of a large publisher. While they may still struggle to get print books into bookstores (not impossible, but difficult), they can make up for those lost sales with the increased royalties from digital self-publishing.

As e-books exploded towards the end of 2010, and that growth continued into 2011, many trade-published writers began to realize they could make more money from self-publishing.

If we take a typical advance of $10,000, that's all most trade-published writers will see from that book. However, if they self-publish and price at $2.99 they only need to sell 5,742 copies to cover costs (assuming a production cost of $2,000) and match the advance. Any copies sold over that amount put the author well ahead, especially considering that e-books never get pulled from the shelves.

As mentioned in the last chapter, in February 2011, e-books became the top-selling format, capturing 29.5% of the market. This was a watershed for many writers and even some with successful careers in trade publishing began running the numbers and seeing what they could make from self-publishing.

Many established writers are continuing with their traditional contracts for books still in print and digitizing their backlists that have fallen out-of-print. Once an author does that, and realizes how much they can make from self-publishing, their traditional publisher has to work harder (and spend more) to keep them happy.

The Case against Big Publishing

A large publisher brings a lot to the table: expertise, experience, editing, marketing, and design. However, these are all things a writer can outsource for a flat fee (and publishers often outsource them anyway).

The Unique Selling Point (or USP) of a trade publishing house is their ability to print lots of books cheaply and get them into lots of bookstores. That's the *real* reason a writer hands over a huge chunk of his or her royalties to a traditional publisher.

However, with print in terminal decline and bookstores on the way out, this USP is becoming less valuable by the minute. When everyone is buying e-books instead of print books, why sign away a percentage of royalties for producing one when doing so is relatively easy? Plus, if you don't want to do the work yourself, many companies out there can take care of everything for less than $2,000.

To those who say they can't afford the upfront costs, consider this: can you afford to give a publisher 52.5% of your royalties *forever* for something you could get done for a one-off payment of under $2,000?

Now, just let me stress that the industry hasn't quite reached this point yet. The majority of sales are still in print and the majority of those are off-line. But it's coming, and faster than you think.

David Gaughran

Why Most Publishers Will Go the Way of Travel Agents

It probably never crossed the minds of most travel agents that the internet would put them out of business. They thought the public needed them to sift through all of the information available and find them the best flights and holiday packages. They thought that airlines, hotels, and resorts were reluctant to deal directly with the public and that people wanted an expert's reassurance to guide them through the process.

It turned out that travel agents weren't such experts after all. Flights were often subcontracted out to charter airlines with terrible service and awful punctuality. Hotels that appeared pristine in the brochure turned out to be cockroach-infested building sites.

Once online booking engines and review sites became popular, people could search for the cheapest deals (not the one the agent was getting kickbacks for) and read what other people—real people—thought of the products. Travel agents were blown out of the water.

Sound familiar? Publishers have had a near-monopoly on the production and distribution of books for centuries. Not anymore. Yet still they continue to resist change, and in doing so, believe and promulgate a number of fallacies.

They think people *want* them to curate selections. They think people rely on their *expertise*. They think people are willing to pay *extra* just because a book has a certain imprint. They're wrong!

Aside from certain imprints in niche genres, the average reader rarely knows or cares who published a book. What they care about is whether it is any good. If a self-publisher has a striking cover, exemplary editing, clean formatting, and an enticing blurb, their work is *indistinguishable* from a trade-published offering. The only real difference is that a trade

54

publisher, with all those overheads, will never beat a self-publisher on price.

The Future

I don't think trade publishing will disappear. Travel agents still exist, albeit mostly in specialized niches. I see the future for trade publishers as dealing with print as a subsidiary right, spinning off print deals for the more successful self-published authors, and producing beautiful, limited edition hardbacks for collectors and super-fans.

With fewer overheads than large publishers, smaller presses have the ability to react to change more quickly (and some have). They might prosper as a result. But for the major publishers, the future looks bleak. Some will survive in one form or another, but many will flounder and eventually go under.

11. Self-publishing Myths

Part of my mission in creating my blog and in publishing this book has been to dispel some of the many myths surrounding self-publishing. One of the most asinine is that those who self-publish never make any money.

The usual reasoning given for perpetuating this myth is that most self-published work is crap and that readers, because they know this, avoid self-published works. According to the myth-makers, self-published books are poorly formatted with terrible covers, no editing, and worst of all, are unfit for public consumption.

Another myth is that even if you're an author with a well-written story and are able to leap over all of these pitfalls to produce a professional-looking e-book, readers will never be able to find it in the sea of crap that's out there. As a result, you are destined to sell only a handful of copies to family and friends.

I come across this misconception all the time—usually from people who either work in trade publishing, those who already have a publishing deal (and have no interest in self-publishing), or those who are pursuing one.

Several elements in the above argument need to be separated.

There Is a Lot of Crap Out There

I don't deny that a lot of self-published books are poorly written, badly edited, or unprofessionally published, and I don't think anyone does. There may be a good story in there somewhere, but the writer has not taken the time to learn how to write, or how to format, or hasn't employed a professional editor to rid the work of even the most basic errors.

Or maybe they have, but no-one will ever read their story because the cover looks like it was done in five minutes on Photoshop. Or maybe they have done all the right things, but the story still simply isn't strong enough.

There are nearly a million items in the Kindle Store, but the truth is I have no idea what percentage of it is crap, because it doesn't matter.

The Amount of Crap is Irrelevant

Now we're getting to the core of this myth, the false assumption everything else rests on—that the amount of crap out there will "taint" even a good writer.

First of all, do self-publishers have some kind of "S" branded on their foreheads? I don't think the average reader knows whether a book is self-published or not if the work is professionally presented. While some imprints or small presses might have a loyal fan base, I don't think the same can be said for the average imprint.

How many imprints and small presses are there in the US alone? How many readers are familiar with even 5% of them?

The purveyors of this myth say it's easy to spot self-published work because of the aforementioned poor presentation or poor writing. But, if you have a quality cover, a great editor, perfect formatting, and a good story, your work cannot be readily distinguished from a trade-published book.

Second, the idea of the poor self-published work contaminating the rest is clearly rubbish. Will my perfectly formatted e-book become corrupted by sharing a virtual bookshelf with the poorly formatted work of a sloppy self-publisher? Will the colors bleed from my cover? Will I begin to misplace my modifiers? Will my characters turn to cardboard? Of course not.

The defenders of this myth usually respond as follows: the mountain of crap makes it impossible to find the few good self-published books.

How Do Readers Find Books?

Self-publishing has been around in one form or another since the invention of ink, but since the launch of Kindle Direct Publishing (KDP) in 2007, it is now easier (and cheaper) than ever both to self-publish and to match the digital distribution of a trade publisher.

Because of this there has been a marked increase in the number of self-published books. The myth-believers argue that this increase (of what they believe is mostly crap), makes it difficult for readers to find the few good books.

These people seem to view Amazon as some kind of giant warehouse in which confused readers wander the aisles, flicking through piles of poorly published dreck. They worry readers will eventually tire of their hunt for quality and leave the store without purchasing anything. This clearly has no basis in reality.

Even before KDP launched there were several million books available on Amazon. How did readers find new great books? The same way they always have: telling each other. The primary reason readers buy a particular book is because they have read and enjoyed something by the author before. The secondary reason is that it was recommended from a trusted source, such as a friend, colleague or reviewer.

The only thing that has changed is that "telling each other" has gotten much easier. People review books on Amazon or Goodreads, book bloggers share discoveries with the world, people tweet their favorites or post links on Facebook, they e-mail each other, they press a book into a friend's hand and say: "You *have* to read this."

It doesn't matter if there are 10 self-published books, or 10 million, people will still find books the exact same way—by telling each other. I don't have any problem finding good books. Do you?

You Will Only Sell to Family and Friends

I have a little secret to share: your family and friends won't buy that many copies. I don't mean this in a bad way. I don't expect anybody to purchase my books, although I am grateful to anyone who does, but most of my friends and relatives either haven't made the switch to e-books yet or don't want to. I can't expect them to do that just for me.

In any event, family and friends help and support in endless ways that are infinitely more valuable than simply purchasing books; I wouldn't trade that for thousands of sales.

What I found is that family and friends are great at getting the word out and helping you make a little noise around your book's release. Those supportive relatives and acquaintances who do purchase tend to do so only in the first few days post-release; after that, you are on your own.

You Will Never Make Any Money

So if friends and family won't buy your book, who will? Readers. Why? Because readers love new books. If they didn't, Shakespeare, Austen, and Dickens would top the charts all of the time.

My first release, a short story, outsold "Metamorphosis" by Franz Kafka—one of the all-time great short stories—for the first few days it was on sale. Most people I meet haven't read Kafka's short story so there is no way the market for it is saturated. There is also no way that my story is better, but it does have one advantage—it's newer.

People love discovering new writers and new stories, and they love sharing their discoveries. As long as you tell people your book is there, as long as you promote it beyond telling your family and friends, you have a chance. Readers will hear about your book, either from a friend, or a review, or one of your promotions on a forum, or on Facebook, or on Goodreads, or on Twitter, and they will check it out. If they like the cover, they will read the blurb. If they like that, they will read the sample. If they like the sample they may purchase the book. If they enjoy the read, they will tell more people. This is word-of-mouth, and it's the only thing that has ever really sold books.

Just this morning I got a message from a stranger who had heard about my book (somehow), and decided to purchase it. They enjoyed it so much, they wrote a lovely review (my sincere thanks to them).

Their blog seems to get a decent amount of traffic, and there is a good chance someone else will read this review and decide to check out my book. This is how word-of-mouth works. I've no idea how they first heard of my book, but now they are telling other people to buy it.

So, what chance do you have of enough readers telling others to lead to enough sales to break even, let alone make a profit? The fact is, achieving success is very difficult. Out of all the writers who want to make a living from writing, the percentage of people who do is very small. This is true whether you self-publish or pursue a trade deal. It's a tough game. But if you write a great story, present it well, and tell people about it, you have a chance.

The myth-peddlers would have you believe that only a handful of writers, such as Hocking, Locke and Konrath, are making a success out of self-publishing, and that they are anomalies. Everyone else, they suggest, is doomed to fail. Not so.

In *Part Three* of this book I present the success stories of 33 self-published writers in their own words. Most are selling more than 1,000 copies a month; some of are selling more than 1,000 copies a *day*!

Most have no history in trade publishing and had no platform initially. When you hear these writers speak about their self-publishing experiences, one after the other, the effect is extremely inspiring—and it's the best possible response to the naysayers.

12. It's a Great Time to Be a Writer

In 2011, self-publishing went mainstream. It's not unusual to see a news report or read an article in the *Financial Times* on an indie best-selling author who has snagged an agent or signed a trade deal, or even coverage of the self-publishing scene in general.

Even so, some self-publishers complain they aren't shown respect from the trade publishing community but are treated with disdain or condescension (others don't care). There have been numerous heated discussions, spats, and bickering on forums with trade published authors on one side and self-publishers on the other. We *should be* on the same side, working together to advance our collective interests, but sometimes self-publishers are viewed as the enemy, or wayward children that are making a terrible mistake.

What some trade-published authors (and those who aspire to be) don't realize is that the increasing success of self-publishing is good for all writers. Let me explain.

Some writers simply have no interest in self-publishing. They don't want to learn the new skills necessary, they have little or no interest in producing e-books, and they can't imagine operating without the support network a trade deal provides. Many doubt they could hire people to do as professional a job on their book as a trade publisher does, and some simply don't have the time (or resources) to set themselves up as a self-publisher.

Others point to the fact that print is still more than 70% of the market, and if there is one thing trade houses do well, it's sell quantities of print books to bricks-and-mortar stores.

Many authors have doubts about how many books they could sell on their own.

That's fine, and these are all valid reasons for sticking with trade publishing. In fact, in the short-term at least, I think the most successful writers will be those who combine self-publishing and trade-publishing to maximize their income and their exposure to all sectors of the market.

I think many self-publishers would consider a trade deal, depending on the terms, and I think a lot of trade-published writers have thought of self-publishing on some level, or at the very least are keeping an eye on developments.

However, some trade-published writers are dead against self-publishing and react negatively to every "good news" story about self-publishing they see. These traditionalists are concerned that the rising popularity of e-books will only swell the self-publishing ranks.

But what a lot of these writers don't realize is that the rise in self-publishing is good for them too. If you are a trade-published writer with no interest in self-publishing, the increased viability of self-publishing is good for you. If you are an aspiring writer whose only desire is to be published by a trade house, the rise in self-publishing is good for you too. Why? Leverage. Every writer knows that when an agent is submitting a book the best case scenario is to have a number of offers on the table. Terms tend to get better when there is more than one offer available as the agent plays the publishing houses off against each other to get the best deal. That's their job. That's business.

With up to 70% royalty rates available through self-publishing, from now on, every time an author negotiates with a publishing house, the publisher will know that the author has another option. Even if that option is one you never intend on exercising, the publisher does not know that. All they know is that more and more writers are considering self-publishing and will continue to consider it as the e-book market grows.

Clever agents and authors are already factoring this into negotiations. Before, the writer with only one offer was faced with a difficult choice: accept the (often crummy) offer on the table or risk losing it by gambling on another round of submissions. Of course, a smaller-than-hoped for advance translates into a smaller print run and a smaller promotional push—a vicious circle that makes the job of selling enough books to get a better deal next time very difficult.

But this has all changed. Now, each time a writer or agent enters into talks with a publishing house their hand is *automatically* enhanced, because they have the option of playing the self-publishing card. Large publishers know that self-published writers can earn up to four times the royalty rate offered by them. Publishers know there are more ways than ever for writers to produce professional books and get them into the hands of readers. Publishers know self-publishing is often a viable, and in some cases lucrative, option for any writer.

This is good for *all* writers. Every trade-published writer will have one extra "offer" on the table to use as leverage. And the more offers you have, the better chance you have to get a good deal. It's great time to be a writer.

It's Not Either/Or

Some people—and both indie evangelists and arch-defenders of trade publishing are guilty of this—seem to think that self-publishing and trade publishing are mutually exclusive paths. This nonsense needs to be dealt with immediately.

There are many authors who have trade deals but are also self-publishing other titles. There are also plenty of authors who are self-publishing but are pursuing trade deals. Some authors with long careers in trade publishing (which they don't intend abandoning) are only self-publishing reverted backlist titles.

You can't squeeze writers into boxes. Life is often more

complex than simple definitions allow, and the publishing industry is becoming more complex every day.

The old, linear publishing value chain has changed forever. In the past, every cog in the publishing machine had its place. Content went from author to agent, to publisher, to distributor, to retailer, to reader. Money (more or less) went in the opposite direction.

Now, that has all changed. Publishers are cutting out agents and going direct to authors to publish backlists. Agents are becoming publishers. Publishers are moving into retail. Retailers are becoming distributors and publishers. Authors are publishing themselves and are selling direct to readers, becoming their own distributors and retailers.

People who see self-publishing and trade publishing as mutually exclusive paths are failing to grasp this new complexity. In a world that is becoming increasingly chaotic, the spoils will go to those who are nimble and adaptable. The last thing you should do is weigh yourself down with unnecessary ideology.

Take the deal that will make you the most money, or that has the best terms, or that brings you closer to your goals. Don't turn down a deal, or accept a deal, out of misplaced loyalty to one creed or another. It is your job to get the best deal possible for yourself. No-one else is going to do it for you.

I've found that I love the self-publishing community. I love the atmosphere, the way everybody helps each other, and that everyone has time to school a beginner. That doesn't mean I wouldn't take a trade deal if the terms were right. I would be foolish to close that door.

If you have already decided to self-publish at least some of your work, here's what you can look forward to: greater engagement with readers; complete creative control over how your work is presented; a price that you set; four times the standard book industry royalty rate; and the support of an entire community as you take your first steps.

The most satisfying aspect? The freedom to write whatever you like and publish it when it's ready. It's a great time to be a writer.

PART TWO: DIGITAL SELF-PUBLISHING

Now that we have covered *why* you should self-publish, we are going to look at *how*: everything from writing your story, designing your cover, getting your story edited, formatting your work, uploading and pricing, as well as a whole range of marketing tools, such as websites and blogging, social media, reviews and promotion, as well as how to address a sales slump.

The Biggest Mistake Self-publishers Make

On my blog, and throughout this book, I make the point that if self-publishers want to have *any* chance of success they have to present their work in the most professional manner possible. That means an eye-catching cover designed by a professional, spending money on a professional editor, formatting an e-book correctly, and conducting yourself appropriately when marketing your novel.

Many self-publishers skip some or all of these steps. As a result, there is a lot of poorly presented work out there. On the other hand, you can follow all of the steps to the letter and still fall flat, with either poor sales or poor reviews killing your career before it even had a chance.

How? Publishing before you are ready. According to editors and agents, the number one mistake new writers make is sending out a manuscript before it is ready.

In the past, the writer only had two real choices. Revise it, or write something new. Now there is a third choice: self-publish it. I think it's amazing that writers now have a way to bypass agents and huge publishing conglomerates and achieve virtually the same reach (in terms of e-books) just by publishing through a few websites.

I'm also a huge fan of the control it gives the writer over every aspect of the publishing process. Writers can decide how their story is presented, and at what price it should sell. They can also decide whether something gets published at all. This is a huge responsibility. Writers, for their own sakes, must use it wisely.

Now that I have built up something of an audience, it

kills me every day that my historical novel *A Storm Hits Valparaíso* is not yet on sale. I have huge plans for this book when it eventually becomes available to the public. However, I also want my readers to get my best possible work. If I put out sub-standard stories, readers will never buy another book with my name on it. If I put out great stories, they will read everything I publish. I could publish my novel now and I'm sure it would do okay. I have had lots of people read early drafts and tell me they really enjoyed it. But it's not ready. I know it can be a lot better. I owe it to myself (and my readers), to keep working on it until it is. Self-publishers need to be very disciplined. They need to look beyond the short-term sales potential and consider that every release helps build a career, and a writer can only build a career if their readers keep coming back for more.

So how do you know when your work is ready for prime-time? That is tough, it really is. Writers are the worst judges of their own work. Writers tend to think everything they write is crap or everything they write is amazing, often holding both opinions simultaneously (and without contradiction). It takes confidence in your abilities to write something, but you need a critical eye to edit it effectively. This dichotomy can cause writers to undervalue or overvalue their work (or swing between the two). You need to have beta readers who are able to be honest with you. More importantly, you need to be honest with yourself.

When I am done with *A Storm Hits Valparaíso*—however long it takes—I know I will be able to publish it, stand behind it, and say proudly: "This is my best work." Make sure you can say the same.

Step 1: Write Your Story

This goes without saying, right? Don't let yourself be distracted by all the other tasks you have to learn—cover design, marketing, formatting, pricing, or social media. After all, if you don't have anything to sell, you can't make any money.

Most of the top-selling indie authors have numerous titles, sometimes across different genres, and often including shorter work as well as novels. I'm planning to publish a series of short stories and collections, as well as a number of novels. Set your own goals.

Forget all those shiny new toys you have to play with; Twitter, blogging, Facebook and all of the rest can be huge time-sinks. Make sure you set aside time for writing every day. That time is golden. You should aim to be producing new work on a regular basis. It's this content that people will buy (and will hopefully want more of), so don't let the process of publishing distract you from regularly sitting down and writing. Every day.

If you want to be a professional writer (that is, make money out of it), you have to have a professional attitude. Be disciplined.

Write the Story You Want to Read

Many writers hate being asked where they get their ideas because the answer is obvious. They *make them up*. The most common cliché doled out to newer writers is "write what you know." This isn't bad advice, but it is limiting advice. If you were a CIA field operative during the Cold War, you might have a gripping spy novel in you, but what if you weren't? I've never fired a musket, eaten a horse, or had sex with a sailor, but I'm pretty sure I could imagine what these feel like. And if you can imagine it, you can write about it. So while you can, by all means, write what you know, you can also write the story you want to read. If your bookshelves are filled with detective novels, maybe you should reconsider your plan to write fantasy. If you are serious about writing you should also be reading regularly in your genre.

If you love reading thrillers and have the perfect concept for a new series but think you should be writing literary fiction, think again. Write the book *you* want to read.

Sending Your Story Out into the World

So your story is finished. Are you ready to publish? Not quite. It's always good to let a story stew for a week or two (several in the case of a novel) before you check it over again. This distance allows you to put aside the emotional connection you have to it as the writer, and attempt to read it as a reader first would. In the meantime, write another story—that's your job.

When you are ready, I suggest printing out the story and editing on paper. You will be surprised at how many more errors you spot on a printed page compared to on-screen. Reading your work aloud is another clever way of catching clunky phrasing or awkward dialogue. When you are done with that, leave your manuscript another few days or weeks, then read it again.

As you gain more experience in writing and self-editing, you'll get a better sense of when a book is ready to be sent out into the world.

Getting a Second Opinion

Done yet? Nearly. You need at least one more pair of eyes (in the form of a beta reader) to look over your manuscript. I guarantee you that a dedicated, competent beta reader will catch some errors, because an objective reader will see things the writer can't.

Your beta reader can be anyone you like, but it should be someone who has good literacy skills and can offer you more than a simple thumbs up or thumbs down. Essentially, your beta reader is a "stand-in" editor, helping you clean up your text before you submit it to a professional so that you minimize your editorial costs. You need your beta reader to assess your use of grammar, your sentence structure, your word usage, and so on, and also to advise on whether your story works, your characters are engaging, and your plot (and subplots) are resolved successfully.

Fellow writers often make the best beta readers. If you don't know anyone suitable, writers' forums are a good place to find willing beta readers and may also provide password-protected areas where you can post work and ask for feedback. While this can be useful for determining whether something works in a very general sense or for providing you with basic critiques, I find it more fruitful to develop a relationship with a beta reader who allows you to e-mail your work to them for constructive criticism.

Remember, don't abuse your beta reader! Send them only your most polished work. But you knew that already, right?

Step 2: Design Your Cover

Let's face it, everyone judges a book by its cover. If you have an ugly cover, people may never read your story.

There are certain conventions in book design—play with these at your peril. A reader selecting a title depicting a cartoon blonde overburdened with shopping bags and teetering on stilettos is not expecting free-form poetry.

If you set false expectations, your sales will suffer. George R. R. Martin's epic fantasy series *A Song of Fire and Ice* nearly never got off the blocks. For the first book in the series, *A Game of Thrones*, the designer opted for something a little different, and sales were muted.

Thankfully, his UK and Australian publishers went for a more traditional fantasy cover, and the international success of the series convinced his US publisher to stick with it. It has since sold 7 million copies worldwide. Make no mistake: design matters.

Every genre has its conventions, whether science fiction, thriller, detective novel, or romance. Literary fiction allows a little more latitude but tries to avoid looking like a "genre" book. Make sure you have a good idea of what is standard for your genre.

The stigma attached to self-publishing, although not as widespread as it once was, exists partly because many of the covers of self-published books appear unprofessional. You don't want to put people off before they even get a chance to sample your writing. Also, remember that your self-published work won't just be up against other indie authors—you have to compete with the rest of the publishing world too.

If you are a graphic designer, great, do the cover

yourself; if not, hire one, preferably a designer with experience in book cover design. This, along with professional editing, is one of the very few areas where you should spend money. It's worth it: a bad cover can sink a book.

Most writers know this deep down, which is why some publishing contracts include a clause stating that the author has final approval over the cover. Unfortunately, in practice, more often than not the trade-published author has little say over cover design. This is either because they are left out of the loop until the final possible moment, creating pressure on them to quickly approve the design rather than risk delaying the book's scheduled release and nixing planned promotional efforts, or because their opinion is not valued as they are not design professionals.

Designers simply don't have time to read every book and often only get a blurb or synopsis to work from. While cover designers do their best, they also need approval on the cover design from marketing and editing. So many fingers in the pie can often result in a cover the writer is unhappy with but can do little about.

When self-publishing, you have none of these concerns. You can do whatever you like. Be sure you use that power wisely.

To ensure you end up with something you're happy with and don't harass your designer with endless revisions, which will cost you money and make them hate you, it's important to give your designer as much information as possible.

Give them a copy of your book, and because they may only flick through the book, give them a blurb too. Tell them exactly what you are looking for and don't just say "something fresh." You can use examples or provide copies of covers you like. Spend time looking at best-selling covers; there are plenty of websites out there that collate them. Make note of what you like and don't like and explain these features to your designer. The more information you can give, the better chance there is of the designer coming up with something that appeals to you.

You will find excellent tips on cover design in the *Resources* section at the end of this book, but there are two crucial elements of e-book cover design you must be aware of.

Your cover must look good as a thumbnail. Most people will only see your cover on search listings. Images are pretty small, maybe one inch by half-an-inch, so keep images clear and fonts big. It also should look good as a grayscale image, as many readers will be browsing for books on their Kindles. In short, keep it simple. Keep radical or ornate design for a print version. We're talking about e-books. They're not going to be on anyone's coffee table.

In an effort to keep costs down, I had my sister—a book cover designer for a UK publisher—do a little moonlighting for me. That might seem like cheating, but you must use whatever advantage you have to publish as cheaply as possible. The less you spend, the less you have to sell to cover your costs; everything after that is profit—forever. You want to get to that point as quickly as you can.

There are tips on how to find a designer in the *Resources* section, but whomever you choose, make sure you see samples of their work first. If you are on a tight budget, try sticking up a poster at your local art college. A student designer, keen to build his or her portfolio, may do your cover at a reduced price or in exchange for something you can provide (like copy for their website), and you might be pleasantly surprised at the results.

Whatever you decide, make sure your designer is aware you will need two files. One is actually inserted into the e-book and one is the cover displayed on the sites, and they have slightly different specifications.

The e-book file should be 600 by 800 pixels and can be a JPEG, TIFF or PNG file. The cover file should be a minimum of 500 pixels wide and a maximum of 1280 pixels tall, and must be a JPEG or TIFF file for Amazon, and Barnes & Noble only accept JPEGs. They should be saved at 72 DPI for optimal web-viewing, and with images displayed in RGB color mode. Retailers will compress your images when displaying them so they should have minimal compression to begin with. Also, for a pale-colored cover, it's best to outline with a narrow (3 or 4 pixel) border in medium gray to define the boundaries, as it can get swallowed up in all the white space. Don't worry if you don't know what any of that means; your cover designer will.

Most importantly, make sure your designer knows what you are looking for, and don't be afraid to reject a design you're not happy with. This is the "face" of your book. Make sure it looks good.

Step 3: Edit Your Story

Now that your cover has attracted readers, they will want to sample your writing, so you better make sure your book has been professionally edited.

If you don't engage a professional editor, you will regret it. Most readers sample a work first and most e-book retailers allow them to download a chunk for free to decide if they want to buy. The size of the sample is around 10% on Amazon, but can be larger on the other sites.

In *Part One*, we talked a little about the importance of editors. If you have errors in your work (and you will, no matter how clean you think your prose is), readers will spot them, and some have been known to leave scathing reviews of books they have only sampled.

Even if readers buy your book without sampling it first, if they find errors they will not only point them out in the reviews section of your book page but will also be wary of buying anything written by you again. Not a great business plan, but surprisingly some writers do this all the time. The absolute worst thing you can do is publish something that is unedited or poorly edited.

All writers, no matter how talented, no matter how firm their grasp of grammar, need editors. Hire one or you will regret it.

Now that we are clear on that, how do you go about getting an editor? Again, as for your cover designer, a personal recommendation is the best way to go. Many self-published writers plug the services they use on their blogs and websites. If you are a fan of a self-published author, check out their site to look for a mention of their editor.

Failing that, writers' forums are great resources to help you find editors and to warn you about scammers, and there are dedicated sites such as Writer Beware which warn against the unscrupulous and incompetent. More information is included in the *Resources* section at the end of this book.

American writers may notice that editorial rates in the UK are cheaper, but unless your book is primarily aimed at the UK market, I recommend you stick to a US editor or at least one with experience editing for the US market.

Before handing over any money, check the editor out thoroughly. Some scam artists or inexperienced operators may take novices for a ride, wasting their limited resources and producing bad work.

Ask editors for testimonials, check their credentials, and check them out on writing forums. I would also advise authors to agree rates in advance, and, most importantly, get a sample edit before paying for anything. Most dedicated editors provide a free sample edit or critique of 1,000 words or so—if they don't, avoid them.

Every editor, like every writer, has a different style. A sample edit will allow you to determine whether you can work together effectively. Don't send the editor a "doctored" version of your manuscript with mistakes added to "test" them, but likewise don't send them only the cleanest chapter that you've pored over a hundred times if the rest of your work isn't as professionally presented. Send your chosen editor a realistic sample of your manuscript as it stands, because he or she will use that to establish how long your edit will take them. Some editors will ask you to send the entire manuscript before they can quote, for that reason.

I strongly advise against trying to save time by skipping the self-editing process or by dispensing with beta readers because you figure an editor should clean everything up anyway. The more your editor has to correct, the longer it will take and the more it will cost you. Plus, your editor can only work with what you send him or her; a polished turd, after all, is still a turd. There are several different kind of edits, but I will talk about the two most relevant in this section.

Manuscript Appraisal

A manuscript appraisal may not be applicable for all writers, but it's worth mentioning. If you're unsure whether your novel is working or need general advice on structure, characters, plot holes, or whether your manuscript is ready for publication, I suggest you get a manuscript appraisal. Keep in mind, however, that a manuscript appraisal does not usually include a sample edit and your novel will not be ready for publication after receiving an appraisal. It is simply a critique of your work with some editorial suggestions and you will still have a lot of work to do to address the concerns raised. Your manuscript will, therefore, need further editing following an appraisal.

For a normal-sized novel (80,000 to 100,000 words) an appraisal usually costs between $300 and $600. In return, you receive a 10-page (or so) report on what is working and what is not. The editor should provide plenty of examples from your novel to illustrate their points, but will not fully mark-up your manuscript to point out each error.

If your work is more polished or you are beyond the point of needing large-scale structural advice (and self–editing and good beta readers *can* get you beyond that point, depending on your level of skill and experience), what you need is a copy editor.

Copy-editing

Copy editors check your grammar, punctuation and spelling to correct run-on sentences, comma splices, excessive comma use, typos, and other errors. What a copy editor usually will not do (at least not in any great detail) is point out that your story isn't working, that your characters are not engaging, that your ending is weak, or that your plot doesn't make sense. *Some* will, but ideally, these are issues you should have already weeded out with your beta-readers.

Copy-editing is usually charged by the hour or by the page. Hourly rates can be anything from $35 an hour up to $200 an hour, depending on the pedigree of the editor involved (although the rate is no guide to the quality of the editor in and of itself). Page rates may range from $5 a page to more than $25 a page. The lower end of the spectrum still has many fine editors (although research and referral are key here). The higher end will usually be made up of those who have edited bestsellers and prize-winners, which has allowed them to raise their rates.

When you contact an editor with your project and explain what you are looking for and your level of experience, they will usually tell you their hourly (or page) rate, ask you the total word or page count, and give you an estimate of their fee. It's only an estimate—the editor doesn't know how clean or riddled with errors your manuscript will be, although, again, the sample edit will be a useful guide for both of you. While it's often normal to pay in advance for a manuscript appraisal, for copy-editing you commonly pay some money in advance and the rest on delivery.

Please don't make the mistake of sending an editor work that isn't ready. It should have been self-edited by you over several drafts (especially if you are starting out), and it should have been torn apart by your beta readers and put back together again by you (then approved by your beta readers again). If you don't know what I am talking about, or you are not convinced, go back and read Chapter 5 again. Believe me, self-editing before having your work edited will save you bundles of money and a world of heartache in the long run.

Some of you might be tempted to have a friend edit for you. Even if they have a Masters in English Literature, work for a newspaper, are a published writer, or whatever, I strongly urge you to reconsider. Professional editing is essential.

Yes, you have to pay for it, and yes, it's expensive, but remember you're asking readers to pay for your work, so you better give them a professional product that's worth the money. I've said it before, but I'll say it again: if you want to be successful, treat writing and self-publishing as a *business*.

I decided to begin by self-publishing some short stories. It proved an excellent way to learn the ropes and I highly recommend it. My plan was to publish a series of "singles" for 99c, then bundle collections of five together for $2.99.

My first release, *If You Go into the Woods,* was two short stories bundled together. Both stories are quite short (about 2,000 words each), and I think 4,000 words is the absolute minimum readers expect for 99c, so I published them together.

The first story had been already published (and thus edited) by two different magazines, but the second story needed a copy-edit. Again, I did my best to keep my costs down. I contacted an editor I knew through a writers' forum and explained my project. She quoted me her rates and I sent her the first story, which she agreed to do as a sample edit. I was satisfied with her approach and the results, so I sent her the second story.

The cost for editing a short story will work out between $60 and $150, depending on how clean it is and how long it is. It usually works out cheaper to send a whole collection at once. If this sounds like a lot for short stories, remember you will be able to sell stories individually and in collections. When you bundle them together you will incur no extra editing costs (as all of them will have been edited and released separately at first), and you might even be able to use one of your existing covers with slight modifications.

Novels, of course, are much longer and more expensive to edit. You may hear rates quoted from anything as low as

$200 right up to $5000 and beyond. You need to be careful here because a bad edit can be worse than no edit at all. If the standard rate for a copy-edit is $40 an hour, you can begin to see what kind of edit $200 buys you. Most novels can't be read in five hours, let alone read thoroughly and marked up. Check the editor's credentials and remember that if you want a professional editor, you must pay professional rates. Editing a book takes time. An experienced editor doing a basic copy edit will get through 3 to 7 pages an hour. If your novel is standard length, that's at least 40 to 60 hours work. And that's just the first pass. Most editors will do two (although the second will be quicker). If you find a good editor with experience and testimonials to back up their prices, and you are happy with their sample edit and think you could form a good working relationship with them, then $2,000 isn't too much to pay to have a standard-length novel properly, thoroughly edited by a professional.

Shop around, but don't let price be the only factor in choosing an editor. A good relationship is at least as important, and experience is crucial. Before you balk at these prices, remember this: editing is an investment in your work. Not only that, each time I go through my editor's suggestions and comments I learn something as a writer. You're getting an education as well as a service. Editing is essential, and aside from cover design it is the only thing you have to spend money on. The rest you can do yourself. Don't skimp on editing, it will show.

Step 4: Format Your Story

Different e-readers and devices use different software to display e-books, but there are a few industry standard file formats. As a self-publisher you will need to learn the digital equivalent of typesetting, known as formatting.

I recommend that you start learning how to format while you are waiting for your final edits or your cover design to be completed. You won't be able to begin formatting your e-book until you have the edited file back from your editor, but it's good to get some practice in before then.

E-readers can do several things that printed books can't, but these features make formatting a little tricky. For one, e-books have no "pages," as such. Each e-reader has its own default fonts, font sizes, and other display options each user can customize. To enable this, your e-book must be set up so that everything displays correctly on a variety of different screens, and so that your text flows and wraps correctly when a reader chooses to zoom in or out. If you do it right, e-book formatting looks really neat on any device.

The only real way to learn formatting is by doing it yourself, and you need to be on a computer. To make this easier for you, I have also copied this chapter to a section of my blog (davidgaughran.wordpress.com/formatting) so you can read it while formatting. It has links to download all the software you need and all sorts of extra formatting tips and advice that you can consult while you are actually formatting. That link is also in the *Resources* section.

Formatting 101

There's no easy way to tell you this, but I am going to have to ask you to do something and you're not going to like it. If you want to publish your book, and if you want to the results to look perfect, there is no way around it—you are going to have to do a teeny tiny bit of computer programming.

Alright, you got me, there is a way around it: you can pay someone to do it. But it will cost you a minimum of $100 to $200 to get it formatted correctly, more if it's non-fiction, and more again if it's super-long, has lots of images, or has any other visual/layout quirks you need incorporated. Add more again if you are interested in publishing to Smashwords (and you should be).

If you are still thinking about paying someone to format for you, I have listed some recommended services in the *Resources* section and on my blog, but remember that's more copies of your book you have to sell to cover your costs, which means more time until you break even. Remember, all of your self-publishing costs are sunk costs—once you cover those, everything after that is profit, and you want to get to that point as quickly as possible.

Anyway, we are here to learn. When you get to the point that your time is so valuable it should be spent writing instead, outsource formatting. Until that time, roll up your sleeves and get ready to format.

Guido Henkel's Guide to Formatting

Self-published author Guido Henkel has produced an amazing free guide to formatting your e-book properly. It's a nine-part guide (but you get through it quite quickly, as most of it is patient explanation rather than actual steps you have to take). If you are serious about formatting professionally, you have to read it before you begin. I'll summarize the key points below, but this summary is not a substitute for reading Guido's guide, a link to which is both in *Resources* and on my formatting page (davidgaughran.wordpress.com/formatting). If you are reading this on your e-reader you will need to be on your computer while reading Guido's guide, so you can follow each step as he does it, which is the only way to learn. I do a couple of things slightly differently, but this is just a question of style. All the options are explained in my formatting guide, so you can choose the most appropriate for you.

Even if you own an e-reader, I recommend that you download the free Kindle app for your computer. It's essential for checking your files as you format them. That link is also listed at the end of this chapter. Once you have installed the Kindle app, you can sample Kindle books for free (and see how the formatting looks for both best-selling titles and for your own work).

The Basics

There are no shortcuts! You might hear of shortcuts and think I was unaware of them. But if you try, for example, just to export an e-reader ready file from your manuscript in Microsoft Word, you are asking for trouble. Trust me.

You might also hear about programs such as MobiPocket Creator, which can produce a Kindle-ready file straight from your Word file. You might hear of people who did this and said their formatting was perfect. You might even *be* one of those people. However, this approach can result in problems with your formatting that you may be unaware of.

If you have already formatted some of your work by either of the steps above, you might think what I'm saying is garbage. You might have checked the file you created and seen no problems. However, what you might not realize is that there could be all sorts of hidden HTML code in your files that could cause problems on other e-readers. Your "perfect" e-book might look screwy on an iPhone, a Nook, or a Kobo reader. Also, there is no telling how future e-readers will interpret that extra hidden code, causing you all sorts of problems.

If you want to be 100% sure your e-books will be formatted *perfectly* on all current and *future* devices, you must follow these steps. If you do, you can look forward to the kind of reviews I received when they said, "This is the most professional design—both inside and out—that I have seen since I started reviewing."

Once you undertake these steps you will realize that Microsoft Word is not your friend. All those bells and whistles they have added over the years, the automatic indenting, the "smart" quotes, on the bullet lists, are about to cause you problems.

You are going to have to get into some HTML; there is no avoiding it. If you are smart enough to write a book, you are smart enough to do this. Don't fret. It's not that bad if you take your time and follow the instructions exactly.

You will need some new software, but don't worry, it's simple to use. In Guido Henkel's guide he recommends TextMate for the HTML, which you must pay for and is only available for the Mac. For a free program that can do much of the same tasks try TextWrangler. If you have a PC, I recommend Notepad++ (which is free). You will also require an e-book conversion program called Calibre which is free for both the PC and the Mac.

The Nitty Gritty

There are a whole host of sales channels for your e-book, and to maximize your revenue you should upload to as many of them as you can. Essentially, what you need to produce are three separate documents:

1. A MOBI file for Amazon;

2. An EPUB file for Barnes & Noble (and other retailers if you go direct); and,

3. A *clean* Microsoft Word document for Smashwords.

If you follow Guido Henkel's step-by-step guide you will end up with the MOBI and EPUB files. It took me quite a few painful hours to do my first, but the next time was a breeze. Even something much more complicated—like this book—was less than a day's work.

Smashwords

The clean Microsoft Word document for Smashwords you will have to produce yourself, as Guido Henkel's guide doesn't cover how to format it. It's a frustrating process, essentially about taking out all of the formatting Microsoft Word puts in automatically and re-entering things a different way.

Smashwords has a style guide, available free, to help you through the process. Read it all. It's no page-turner, but you can get through it in less than an hour and it's essential to having your documents accepted by Smashwords.

How quickly you can work through the style guide and convert your document will depend on your level of familiarity with Word. My document took me less than an hour, but only because my editor had cleaned a lot of it up. At worst, it will take you a day—the first time.

Sales on Smashwords aren't big, but it's the only way to get onto Kobo, Sony, and Diesel, and the easiest way to get into the Apple iBookstore, as well as the only way for international authors to get their books on Barnes & Noble. It's also one of the only ways that most international readers (outside of the UK, Ireland, Canada, Australia and Germany) can purchase your work and avoid heavy surcharges (explanation in *Appendix B*). It's worth the hassle.

Testing

Before you begin uploading your files, I recommend testing them as much as possible. As Guido Henkel recommends in his guide, you should be testing the files in your browser as you make changes. When you are done, also test them on a Kindle or the free Kindle app. If you don't have a Kindle, I recommend reducing the size of the screen to mimic one, as some problems with your layout will only become apparent then. I also recommend seeing what it looks like with a larger font size, again to sniff out hidden problems (and because many readers will view this way).

Once your files are ready, you can begin uploading your e-book. Excited yet?

Step 5: Uploading and Pricing

Now that you have all your documents ready, you need to upload your work to the various sites and set the price.

Sales Channels

There are many sales channels for self-published work: Amazon, Barnes & Noble, Smashwords, Kobo, Apple, Sony, Google and Diesel (and romance authors should check out OmniLit).

You should be publishing on all of them, with the possible exception of Google, which I will get to in a moment. Once you have done your formatting, publishing on these sites requires very little work, and if you don't utilize them all you are reducing your potential sales for no good reason.

While Amazon dominates the market, its share is falling and it isn't quite as strong internationally. E-book publishing is a global business worth over $80 billion and you would be foolish to limit yourself to selling only on Amazon. Even in non-English speaking countries there are expatriates and plenty of people who want to practice their English by reading books. It costs you nothing to sell to them too, so you should be doing it if you want to maximize revenue and readership.

I will talk you through the Amazon uploading process in detail below. The rest of the retailers are quite similar, so I will just point out a few quirks. Pricing will be dealt with separately at the end.

Amazon

Amazon controls the majority of the e-book market and sells the Kindle, the most popular dedicated e-reader. Kindle Direct Publishing (KDP) is open to all international writers and you are free to sell your work in all territories for which you hold rights (which will be everywhere, unless you have signed a publishing deal that included the e-rights for certain territories).

Amazon pays a 35% royalty rate across the board, except on sales that qualify for the higher rate. If you price your work between $2.99 and $9.99, you will receive 70% royalties, but only if the customer is in the US, Canada, the UK, Germany, Austria, Switzerland, Liechtenstein, or Luxembourg. Despite some false information out there, it's important to note that it does not matter where the writer is from, they can still receive the higher rate. The territory to which the increased royalty rate applies is expected to expand as KDP rolls out to additional countries, with Spain widely assumed to be next.

Payment is made 60 days after the end of the month in which sales occur and authors are paid by electronic transfer or check, depending on the author's location.

After you open your account with KDP, which only takes a moment or two, you will see a button to upload your book. Once you click on it, you will have to fill out a variety of fields, all of which have clickable explanations. Read them all—they are all pretty straightforward—but I will talk you through some of the less obvious aspects.

Under "Publisher" you can put your own name or that of your publishing company. Whether you want to set up your own company to publish your books is a decision you have to make for yourself. There is a comprehensive discussion of this, and the various tax implications, in the *Practicalities* section at the end of this book. I publish my books through my company, Arriba Arriba Books. I think it looks more professional, but you have to decide for yourself. The book description is crucial. You must take the time to write something enticing and catchy. The best way to learn how to do this is to study the books at the top of the bestseller list, see how they describe them, and use those techniques. You can change all of the information afterwards if necessary, but be aware it could take a few days for the changes to take effect, so it's best to get it right at the start. The book description is what will first sell the book to the reader. Think of the blurb on the back of a print book—write it like that. Make it something people will be excited to read. Make it leap off the page. There is further advice in *Resources*.

Choose the categories carefully because you only get to pick two. Decide which most closely matches your book contents. Amazon will also scan the book and may assign it additional categories; you have no control over that, so choose your two wisely as this will affect which genre bestseller lists you may appear on.

Underneath those, you have the option to select seven keywords that will decide whether your book is displayed under certain searches. Again, choose wisely. Don't pick something too general like "fiction." Try to drill down to something more specific, like "historical fantasy" or "time-travel romance." Think like a reader. Try to guess how your audience would search for books like yours. Amazon will also scan the book's contents and may place you in additional categories. This process is automated.

For the book cover image, as I mentioned in *Step 2*, you need to generate a separate file to the one that actually goes in your e-book. The specifications are mentioned in that chapter, and the additional file should have been provided by your designer. Don't worry if your cover looks funny in the little thumbnail after you upload it, it will look fine on the actual site.

When you get to uploading your book file, you are given

an option to enable Digital Rights Management (DRM). If you don't know what that is, go back and read Chapters 2 and 3, and then decide what to choose. I strongly recommend not enabling DRM, because it can upset your readers. Make sure you then choose to preview your book to catch any formatting issues.

Once you are finished with that page, you will move on to the last step. You should choose "Worldwide rights" to display your book everywhere. You should also enable lending. Pricing will be dealt with separately in the second part of this chapter.

Barnes & Noble

Barnes & Noble is the largest bricks-and-mortar book chain in the US and also have a significant online operation. They make and sell the second most popular dedicated e-reader in America, the Nook, and have the second most popular e-bookstore in the US.

PubIt is their digital publishing platform; however, only writers based in the US may sign up with PubIt. If you can, it's worth going direct. Barnes & Noble pays 65% royalties on all e-books priced between $2.99 and $9.99, and 40% outside of that, and they pay monthly.

International writers can get into Barnes & Noble through Smashwords. However, they receive reduced royalty rates (but only in the $2.99 to $9.99 range) as well as reduced visibility, as Barnes & Noble's algorithms seem to give display preferences to PubIt authors.

Smashwords

Strictly a distributor, rather than a retailer (although you can buy direct from them), Smashwords allows you to publish to Apple, Diesel, Sony, Kobo, and Barnes & Noble. For this, they take a cut of your royalties (after the respective channel takes their cut).

You can also sell direct on Smashwords. Sales are small through their channel, but you have certain options you don't have elsewhere. You can make your work free, you can generate all sorts of promotional coupons, and you can allow readers to sample up to 50% of your work (rather than 10% on Amazon). Royalties are paid 30 days after the end of each quarter by check (US only) or PayPal.

As I mentioned before, they take your Microsoft Word document and use a program to convert it to the various formats they sell. Many writers complain about the formatting the Smashwords system produces and are annoyed they can't upload their own perfectly-formatted files like they can on KDP. However, if you want to list with Smashwords, for the moment at least, you have no choice.

Once you upload your document, your publication will go into a queue for approval. It used to take a couple of days to process the file, but now it's a matter of minutes. When it is done, it will only be on sale on Smashwords itself. To access the rest of the channels you must submit your work to the Smashwords Premium Catalogue and the site will talk you through the various steps. Most important to note is that you need to assign an ISBN number to your book. Smashwords offers a free one, but for the full pros and cons of that please see the *Practicalities* section at the end of this book.

Once you have assigned an ISBN you can apply for Premium Catalogue listing. Before your work can be pushed out to other vendors, Smashwords' staff manually check your file to see if it meets their guidelines. This currently takes around two weeks. Most people get rejected the first few times. Don't panic. It's usually a minor formatting issue that can be easily fixed by referring to their Style Guide. While you await approval, your book will still be on sale on their own site.

Smashwords pays around 60% royalties, regardless of price (with some minor deductions). This means if you are selling outside the $2.99–$9.99 price range, you will get higher royalty rates through Smashwords than through PubIt or Amazon.

US users publishing through Smashwords should turn off the Barnes & Noble distribution channel and publish direct with PubIt, as described above, unless they are publishing 99c books, where they will make more going through Smashwords (but lose some visibility). I recommend experimenting with both to see what works for you. You will also see an option to distribute to Amazon, which indicates that a deal to do so is in the works. This message has been there for quite some time, and nobody is expecting it to happen any time soon (or even at all), so you should switch off distribution to that channel.

The main disadvantage with Smashwords is that, because of how their system works, formatting may not look quite as professional as it does with PubIt and KDP, which enable you to upload your own files. All Smashwords titles must be DRM-free.

Apple

You can publish direct with Apple, but they don't make it easy. You'll need a Macintosh computer, and it's not for the fainthearted. Unless you already know how to publish to Apple, I suggest you publish on Apple through Smashwords.

You will also need an ISBN (which Amazon doesn't require), but Smashwords provides one for free if you publish through them. You still should list with Apple—after all, it costs you nothing—but it definitely isn't worth purchasing a Mac and an ISBN and jumping through all the extra hoops just to list direct.

The iBookstore has potential. There are 100 million iPhones and maybe 25 million iPads out there worldwide, but

Apple doesn't seem to sell a lot of e-books just yet. The biggest effect their entrance into the marketplace has had on Amazon has been to force Amazon to offer higher royalty rates.

This may change (and they have recently improved the intergration with iTunes), but it seems that, at the moment at the least, most iPad and iPhone users seem to use the free Kindle app to purchase e-books. Apple is trying to make it more difficult for their users to buy through the Kindle app, but have so far failed to do so.

Sony, Kobo, Diesel and Google

At the moment, Google's eBookstore doesn't allow authors from outside the US and there are a number of other issues that just make publishing with Google a frustrating experience. Many writers don't bother because Google doesn't seem to sell a lot of books.

If you are considering listing, you should be warned they can discount your books arbitrarily, without your permission and without letting you know. The problem is that Amazon will often automatically price match, which can cause you to drop out of the 70% royalty zone. Remedying this can take weeks, by which time you could be out a lot of money.

There is currently no way to self-publish direct to the rest of these stores unless you have a publishing history with them; you must publish through Smashwords. While sales are small through these channels, Kobo is growing and is making big moves in the international marketplace. They just secured a new round of funding, are opening local-language stores in Germany, France, Italy, Spain, and the Netherlands, and have already made inroads in Australia, New Zealand, Canada, and Hong Kong.

International Writers

There are a few extra challenges international writers have to deal with. All of the abovementioned retailers withhold 30% of your income until you file tax forms with them. The amount of the withheld 30% that will then be released depends on the tax treaty your government has with the US, but for many countries you will get all of it back. There are more details about how to resolve your tax situation in *Practicalities* at the back of this book.

Pricing

There is a lot of debate about pricing. I want to avoid a discussion of the ethics of various strategies here, preferring to talk about the respective pros and cons for the writer employing them.

This means I won't discuss whether it is right for authors to give away work or price it very low (or very high). Let's avoid emotional arguments about how your novel took you three years so it's worth a lot more than $2.99. In a strict business sense, it's worth what people are willing to pay for it. Instead, let's talk about what works and what doesn't depending on your goals.

The only firm belief I have regarding pricing is that you should be flexible. Find the right price for your e-book depending on what you hope to achieve and free of ideology or any other such nonsense. I will, however, outline my pricing strategy and the reasons I have chosen it. Not everyone will agree with my choice. That's fine, you should choose a strategy that suits you.

Maximizing Readers—a Free-for-all

If your primary goal is to maximize readership at the expense of everything else, the best way to achieve this is to give your work away for free. You can do this in several ways, but for an all-encompassing free strategy, upload your work as normal to Amazon and price it at the minimum—$0.99. Then, when you upload to Smashwords, make it free.

Once your book is accepted in the Smashwords Premium Catalogue, the "free" price will be pushed out to all the partners (Apple, Sony, Kobo etc.) and Amazon will reduce its price to $0.00 in a matter of days. They don't tend to reduce the price if it is only free on Smashwords, so you must get into the Premium Catalogue and select distribution to Sony at the very least.

The pros of this strategy are obvious: you get a huge increase in readers. Writers on Kindle Boards have reported going from a handful of sales per month to thousands of downloads. This strategy suits writers whose goal is not to make money but simply to attract readers. That's fine—if that's your goal.

Writers who want to make money hope that readers of the free work will go on to purchase other titles. A lot of these authors have written a series and are hoping the reader will get hooked on the free title and pay for the rest. Others are giving away a short story in the hope their readers will like their writing and pay for longer works.

The obvious downside to choosing to distribute your book free is that you don't get any royalties. On top of that, some people out there will just download anything free so they can say they have 1,000 books on their Kindle. They may never read your book. Finally, one thing to keep in mind is the possibility you are creating a negative value perception of your work. People may assume it's not worth much because you aren't charging for it.

Unfair? Maybe, but it can happen.

Maximizing Readers—99c Pricing

Many authors have success at this price. Some, like John Locke, price all of their work at this price point. Others, like Amanda Hocking, use the first book in a series as bait, price it at $0.99, and charge $2.99 (or more) for the rest. It seems this "baiting" strategy is more effective for a series than for a mixed price range of stand-alone novels. If you are using 99c pricing as part of your overall plan, you should note that the minimum price you can set in Germany is 0.99 Euro (about $1.40) and in the UK it is £0.86 (also about $1.40).

The pros of this strategy are that at this price your work is an impulse buy for a lot of people, so you don't have to work as hard to get them to try it. There are many blogs dedicated to "cheap reads" that will highlight your work, and many Kindle owners exclusively hunt for such bargains.

The cons are that you only get 35c per sale, so to make a living off this strategy you will need to hit numbers only a tiny fraction of writers do. If you have higher-priced work and price low as part of a baiting strategy, you need to get a good portion of readers making the leap to your other work, which doesn't always happen. Also, once you have set a price in your readers' minds—that your novels are worth 99c—it can be hard to get them to adjust upwards. It's possible, but not easy, and you should keep that in mind.

Maximizing Profit

The $2.99 price point seems favored by indie novelists who want to maximize profit. It's the lowest price point for which writers obtain the higher 70% royalty rate, which means they pocket more than $2 per copy sold.

Many writers pricing at $2.99 test out sales at 99c. However, to maintain the same profit, you would need to sell six times the amount of books at that lower price point. Not all do. In fact, some writers have reported an increase in sales when they shifted to $2.99, or, at the very least, an increase in profit. After all, you only need to sell a sixth of the amount to make the same money.

The main advantage, aside from increased royalty rates, is that you have increased flexibility. If your sales drop or you want to run some kind of promotion, you can drop your price. You can't do that at 99c unless you decide to give it away.

Also, at higher price points you can use Smashwords coupons, which can be a very effective marketing strategy. Smashwords allows you to generate unlimited coupons that take a percentage (of your choice) off the price of your work or to sell it at a fixed price (again of your choice) to the coupon holder.

The minimum price is set at 99c. If you already price at that level you can give your work away with a free coupon, but you can't offer a reduction. In other words, you can't generate a coupon offering 20% off.

However, if you are priced at $2.99 you have a range of options with coupons, which can be useful when tied in with a review offer, a blog tour, a competition, or other promotional activities.

The drawback of the $2.99 price point is that you will probably have fewer readers than you did pricing at 99c, even though you are making more money. This means fewer people to tell others they liked your work—and word-of-mouth is crucial for indie authors.

Going Higher

Some authors attempt higher price points. (I'm not talking about deluded writers that price at $12.99 because Dan Brown does and they are *way* better than him.) This is a tricky proposition, but not impossible either. It's all about positioning and perception. If you have a poor cover, bad or nonexistent editing, dodgy formatting, a mediocre sample, or an uninspiring book description, the reader may justifiably think your work is overpriced at $2.99 or even 99c.

However, if you do everything in your power to make your book resemble one from a successful trade publisher—if you run a clever marketing campaign, if you have professionally designed covers, a great opening that readers can sample, a blurb that will hook people in, and your work has been professionally edited—you can price your work at above $2.99 and not only survive but thrive.

Nathan Lowell is a great example of this. While he is not technically a self-published writer, he is one of Robin Sullivan's writers at Ridan Publishing. She self-published her husband Michael's hugely successful fantasy series (and priced them at higher price points) and is now using the same strategy with her other authors. To me, Nathan Lowell's and Michael Sullivan's books look as good, if not better, than anything coming from large publishers. Because of this approach they have been able to price their books at $4.95 (that's a royalty of $3.46 per book), and they have sold truckloads.

The downside, of course, is that higher price points discourage impulse purchasing. Also, the Big Six are experimenting with sales at around $5, which brings you into direct competition with them as well as with the many small presses and e-publishers that price around this point. On the other hand, if you have done everything else right, that could work in your favor. It's all about value-perception.

Flexibility

As I said earlier, the only firm belief I have regarding pricing is that you must be flexible. Decide your pricing strategy, based on your goals, before you publish, but remember it is not set in stone. Don't be afraid to experiment with different pricing for different titles. Basically, find your own "sweet spot."

Even though Robin Sullivan is reasonably committed to higher price points, she has experimented with some titles at $2.99 and $0.99 price points. It worked for Marshall Thomas, but it failed for Michael Sullivan (who ended up selling lots more at $4.95 than at $2.99). The point is, each writer will be different. Each title could be different. Be open to change and you will find a way to maximize your income.

Another writer who has benefited from experimentation is Vincent Zandri. While he is also published by a small press, self-publishers can learn lessons from what StoneGate Ink did for his titles. They priced one of his titles at $0.99, and then after he cracked the Top 10 they jacked the price up to $4.99. Sales dropped but he held on in the Top 100 (selling 800 to 1000 copies a day), making a royalty of $3.49 per copy.

If you are willing to be flexible it could bring you great rewards. Having said that, don't change your book's price too often, Robin Sullivan recommends a minimum of a month at a certain price before you can measure its effectiveness.

My Approach

I have decided on the following price structure (as adapted from Dean Wesley Smith):

Short story singles: $0.99 ($0.35 royalties)
Five-story collections: $2.99 ($2.09 royalties)
Ten-story collections: $4.99 ($3.49 royalties)
Full-length novels: $4.99 ($3.49 royalties)

If I write anything that falls outside those categories (e.g. a novella or non-fiction), I will decide the price on a case-by-case basis, but this is the general structure. Why?

First, I am a short story writer as well as a novelist, and I like to release my shorts on their own. I believe there is a market for them, and my first two titles are doing well.

Second, if you have stories on sale for $0.99 and collections of five for $2.99 (or 60c per story), the collection has a greater perceived value for the reader, and that price point taps into the much higher royalty rate (the same logic applies for collections of 10).

Third, if I build up enough anticipation, and enough of an audience, with my short stories, I might be able to catch enough sales at $4.99 to make them worthwhile. If I get the story right, and the covers, and everything else, it may even seem like a bargain.

Fourth, this strategy allows a lot of flexibility. It's far easier to run a sale for a month and drop your price to $2.99 or even $0.99 from a higher starting point than it is to go in the other direction.

But the key component is flexibility. I don't expect all of my titles to stay in those ranges permanently, that's just the starting point. I will experiment with all sorts of prices (and some free titles) in the future. That way, with hard data rather than hunches, I can find my own sweet spot for each of my titles, which is what this is all about.

I recommend that you define your own strategy, but don't be too rigid. Be prepared to adapt as circumstances change.

Ready to Launch

Your e-book can take up to 72 hours to appear across the various e-bookstore sites. Sometimes Amazon can approve books remarkably quickly (one of my titles went on sale after an hour), so be prepared. More usually, it takes a couple of days. Before you announce your new release to the world, I recommend downloading it yourself and making a final check for errors. The first time you will probably catch one or two.

Once your story appears, congratulate yourself. You are

now a self-published writer. But, by my mother's definition at least, you're not an author yet. To earn that title you need to sell some copies. Be under no illusions: this is where the hard work *begins*.

Step 6: Blogging and Websites

You have written your book, added your cover design, had your work edited, gone through the pain of formatting for the first time, and now everything is uploaded, priced, and available on all of the e-book sales channels. Only problem is, nobody's buying it. Don't worry, you haven't told anybody about it yet, and it takes time to build an audience. Most of the e-book success stories you will read about in the final part of this book took around six months to sell in decent numbers.

The final four steps of this guide will cover your marketing options, all of which will cost nothing but time.

Websites

There are two types of websites: static and interactive. A static website is like this one:

astormhitsvalparaiso.com

This site was designed for me by my friends at Ambient Project. I asked them to set it up in 2009 when I was querying agents, and it hasn't changed since. The idea was that it would act as a kind of calling card, make me look professional, and help agents visualize my manuscript as a real novel for sale. It has a brief description of my novel, thumbnail sketches of the various characters, some historical context, contact information, and a button for visitors to download the first chapter of my book for free.

It costs money to create websites like this (a few hundred dollars for a basic one), but can be a useful tool. However, I would only suggest going down this road if you have a little extra budgeted for marketing. You can achieve some of the same effects with a free page, and you can achieve better effects with a different *kind* of page.

Because a webpage such as that is a *static* page, there is no interaction between the writer and the audience. Readers can't post comments, and you can't post updates without getting in touch with your web designer. While a lot of people visited this page and complimented me on it, the content never changes, so there is no real reason for them ever to return. I have no opportunity to build a connection with my audience and, in the fast-moving world of the internet, a static page, however pretty, is soon forgotten.

Blogging

A blog is an *interactive* page, which can be a great way to connect with potential readers. If there is new content appearing regularly, readers have good reason to keep coming back. Best of all, a blog costs you nothing. I recommend every writer sets up their own blog. Here's mine: davidgaughran.wordpress.com

I use WordPress, but some prefer Blogger, Typepad or LiveJournal; pick the one you are most comfortable with. I think WordPress looks the most professional, but Blogger has its advantages too, especially if you are overwhelmed with the functionality of WordPress.

One thing you should consider purchasing is your own domain name. It only costs around $12 a year and you can use that as the name of your blog instead of a generic WordPress name (like the one I have right now). If your desired domain name is already taken, play with a few variations on your initials, or add your middle name or "writer" to your name—anything, as long as it looks professional. While we are on the subject, if your e-mail address is something like faerygurl456@yahoo.com, jenandtimmy@gmail.com, or spankmenow@hotmail.com,

I'd recommend getting a new one for business.

Layout

Ideally your blog should be clean and easy-to-read. Light text on a dark background might look stylish, but it's awful for extended reading. Keep garish colors to a minimum and make sure any graphics you use are of good quality.

First-time visitors to your blog should be able to find the information they want quickly. You should also have buttons that allow them to share articles they like and to subscribe to your blog. Make a note of other, popular blogs you enjoy and try to replicate their layout.

Building an Audience

While there are more than 2 billion web-users worldwide, there are a *trillion* unique URLs out there and the number of individual web pages increases by several billion every day.

You should update your blog regularly (every day or two if you can) to give people a reason to return. However, they won't come back if they don't like what they see in the first place. You must have something interesting to say because you are using up people's most valuable resource: time.

So what do you write about? Well, whatever interests you, but do try to carve out some kind of niche. If you do it right, and people are coming back to your blog on a regular basis, then you have a captive audience to sell your work to. Don't underestimate the importance of this connection as a sales tool.

I was interested in the fast-moving changes occurring in the publishing industry, and I also wanted to document my own first steps into digital publishing, so blogging about that seemed like a natural fit. However, to be self-critical, my blog does not really reach out to my true book-buying audience, i.e. readers. A blog like mine is enjoyable to write and is great for interacting with other writers and self-publishers, and I am learning a lot from it, but I don't think it's going to boost my sales by much because it doesn't target my readers as much as my colleagues.

This means I will have to compensate for that in my other marketing efforts, but that's fine. It's far better to blog about something you are interested in than to fake it. Readers are smart; they will see through you if you aren't genuine.

I recommend trying to reach out to your readers. If you write cozy mysteries you could have a fan site dissecting the classics. If you are writing a non-fiction book on baseball you could host a discussion on the greatest players and the latest scandals. In truth, your attempts to attract readers don't even have to be that direct. If you blog about great Italian recipes your audience will likely be interested in that romance novel you've set in Sicily. If you write about celebrity gossip, chances are your readers will like the chick-lit book you've written. Even if the subject of your blog is not directly related to your book, if your readers enjoy your writing, they will usually check it out anyway.

One of the keys to building an audience is engagement. People don't want someone to talk *at* them; if they wanted that, they would turn on the radio or watch television. They want someone to talk *with* them. Make sure the comments are open on all of your posts and that you respond promptly. Try to pose a question or two in your articles that will invite discussion. A blog must be an interactive experience, because that's the advantage the web has over a traditional column or published article. If you look at the most popular blogs, the real action is in the comments, and that's what will keep people coming back.

Sommer Leigh has a handy online guide (included in the *Resources* section) for those taking their first blog-steps. But if blogging seems overwhelming, or if you simply have no interest in doing it, don't worry. It's not essential to success.

108

It just means that you will have to compensate in other marketing areas. It's your call.

If you set up your blog properly, you can combine *interactive* and *static* pages. I have static pages for my books and for other information (like my formatting tips) I want readers to be able to find quickly. They act as anchors for the dynamic content. Eventually, my blog will have static pages for each of my e-books as they are released. If you want to get really fancy, you can have a domain name for each book so that if someone types in that web address it will automatically jump to the static page you have set up for that book.

Driving Traffic to Your Blog

It's all very well having the best content in the world, but if no-one sees it in the first place, it's kind of pointless. So how do you get people to come to your blog?

Get your name out there, but be tasteful. Find other writing blogs, or blogs covering a similar subject, and engage with the readers through the comments. If someone sees something thoughtful or interesting, they might check out your blog or even buy your book. I set up a Gravatar/Open ID through WordPress, so on most blogs my picture is beside the comment and my name is a clickable link to the blog.

If you can't interact in a genuine way and choose to self-promote very overtly, you will seem like that guy at the party everyone is avoiding because he's trying to sell insurance. There could be ten people in the room who might be looking for a quote, but if all you talk about is insurance they will quickly tire and move on.

If you seem interesting or knowledgeable when a subject comes up naturally, your audience will be far more likely to consider using your services. Nobody likes the hard sell. Nobody likes a spammer.

Writing Forums

I get good traffic from various writing forums I frequent, but be warned that while no-one reads more than a writer, nothing pisses a writer off more than spam. Be courteous, respectful, and restrict your marketing efforts to the appropriate sections of the forum. I've never checked out the work of another writer who was constantly in my face pushing their book, but I've checked out plenty of books written by people I met and interacted with on forums, Facebook pages or writings sites. A tasteful link in your signature and genuine interaction with others will bring you far better results. Each post will act as a permanent trail of breadcrumbs, leading readers back to your blog and to your books.

Most forums have an area where you can post brief updates from your blog from time to time. However, I have found that most of the clicks I get happen when I am commenting on another topic altogether. Again, if people consider your contributions useful, they are far more likely to visit your blog.

If you are just at the party to blanket the place with business cards, you will be a turn-off. Be a good forum citizen, nobody likes the man with the megaphone.

Google

I'm getting a growing amount of traffic from Google. It takes a while for their search engine bots to find your site and map it, although you can nudge them along by registering your blog with them.

One of the main factors in how a site ranks in Google search results is linkage. If you link to popular sites and they link back, it can have a huge boost on your ranking. The first step you should take is to put a sidebar on your site with links to the big sites/blogs in your subject area. Then, when you comment on their sites (and your name is an automatic link back to your site if you have set it up correctly), it creates pathways between your site and theirs. Google loves these pathways, but assigns more value to links that are actually within posts.

Once more, don't be spammy. If you are visiting high traffic sites just to spread links, it will backfire. Making thoughtful, genuine contributions is what will bring readers back to your blog.

Social Media

By far the easiest and best way to drive traffic to both your blogs and your Amazon listings is by clever use of social media, which I will elaborate on in the next chapter. But you should know that by employing the tips in this chapter, and by promoting my blog through social media using the methods described in the next, I went from next to nothing to 20,000 views a month in the space of 3 months. (Measuring by unique visitors is a truer indication of traffic, but this is the only metric I get from Wordpress.)

There is a lot to learn when it comes to using social media, and it's easy to get distracted by it, but never forget the golden rule: keep writing! The most effective marketing tool for any writer is new work.

Step 7: Social Networking

In the last chapter, I discussed the importance of having a website or blog, and explained the difference between a static page and an interactive page and why the latter is better. Now we're going to talk about signposts, social media, how to connect the dots in your little online world, and how not to behave.

One of the biggest reservations most writers have with self-publishing is a fear their novel will get lost in a sea of titles without a big publisher to trumpet their work. People wonder how their readers can find anything among the million or so items in the Kindle Store and shudder to think what it will be like when there are millions more.

I think anyone worrying about this is looking at it the wrong way. There are more than a trillion unique web pages, yet people have no problem finding (and even buying) items even though billions of new pages get added every day. Despite the amount of junk web pages out there, despite the amount of scammers, e-commerce is booming year after year.

How do people find anything? Signposts. Every link on the web is a signpost to another web page. Google is just a very sophisticated set of interactive, trusted signposts. But anyone can make their own signposts. People talk to each other all the time, helping each other find the good stuff. They e-mail links, tweet them, blog about them, text them. They love sharing signposts. You just need to get some of those signposts pointing to you.

Amazon Author Page

Once you have uploaded your story to Amazon, you should check out Author Central—a tool that allows you to view up-to-date sales rankings for your books, edit the descriptions the customer sees on your book page, and most importantly set up your Author Page. It's a powerful tool and I recommend you exploit it as much as possible.

Readers will see your Author Page when they click on your name in the Amazon listings (search for "David Gaughran" on Amazon to see one that is fully set up). If a reader is interested in your book and is considering purchasing, they often check out the Author Page first. If it sounds interesting, they may give your book a chance. This is another opportunity to hook a reader, just like your title, your cover, your blurb, and your sample. Don't waste it.

Your Author Page displays all of your book titles in one place. You can upload a photo, which is very important because it will then appear on all of your book pages and search listings. You can also link your Author Page up with your Twitter account (showing your latest tweets) and your blog (showing your latest posts), and you can provide a short biographical description. Some authors just list where they were born and the titles of their books. Consider this another blurb which is selling something: you. Make it sound interesting. Note that you will have to set up a separate Author Page for the UK and for Germany, as they don't usually propagate across.

I have noticed quite a bit of traffic going from my Author Page to my blog, and an uptick in Twitter followers. This means I am moving beyond what I described in my last post as networking and actually beginning to reach people who might buy my books. If people like your blog or your tweets, they will stick around—now you are beginning to communicate directly with the people you really want to reach: your readers.

Antisocial Media

If you paused for a moment, like I did, to consider that all of your potential readers will see your tweets and blog posts, that's good. It means you are starting to realize that your online interactions are public and will form an impression in your readers' minds. You want that to be a good impression.

Your blog is not the place to plant flags or settle scores. Your Twitter account is not for chasing chicks or talking about boys. If your Facebook profile is open to the public, please be careful with what you share and what your friends share. It's important to set some dividing lines here. You can have a Facebook Page for business (we'll talk about that below) and a personal Facebook Profile for fun. You can have as many Twitter accounts as you like, but keep one strictly for work.

Think about some of the things your friends or acquaintances might share, and whether that will reflect well on you professionally. My advice is to keep these worlds separate. You may want to switch off sometimes, so it's good to have a personal hideaway.

*Don't Be a D*ck*

If there is one commandment for online behavior, whether forums, Twitter, Facebook, or blogging, it's this: don't be a d*ck.

Don't go on forums to spam people about your book. Don't tweet your new release every hour. Don't use your blog to take on your enemies. Don't turn every conversation into, "That's enough about me, let's talk about you. What do you think of my book?"

In short: don't be a d*ck.

People forget the "social" part of social media. It's about interaction. It's about engagement. This means asking your readers questions and caring about the answers. This means listening to your audience. This means responding to comments in a timely manner. You know, being nice.

As I said before, interaction is one of the key advantages of the web; if you are not leveraging it people will soon change channel—and there are over a trillion channels.

However, if you care about your readers, if you say interesting things to them and encourage them to respond, if you start having conversations rather than giving speeches, readers will come to you. It's the same with Twitter. It's the same on forums. It's the same with Facebook. It's the same with blogging.

Do Unto Others

No-one likes being spammed, friends that only go on about one thing are boring, people who talk and don't listen are annoying, and everyone shuts the door when they see the salesman coming.

There are lots of reasons I buy books, but the only ones I heard about through social networking and actually bothered checking out were written by people who were smart, interesting, funny, had a way with words, offered a different perspective, or were just plain nice.

Twitter

Lots of people have very strong feelings about Twitter. They swear they will never use it, but are worried they will have to. I was one of them, up until three months ago.

None of the things I describe in these marketing chapters are required, and none will guarantee you success. If done right, some of these things may increase your chances of people checking out your e-book. But if your blog is boring, your cover is horrible, your Amazon description is limp, or your sample is poorly written, all of this will be a waste of time.

If you decide not to blog or not to use Facebook, or even to avoid Twitter, that's fine. But you will have to make up for it in other ways. Word-of-mouth is still the most effective way to sell books and nobody can talk about your book if they don't know about it.

With Twitter, the same rules of social media apply but you have to be even more careful because now you have a megaphone. Everything you tweet is publicly available to anyone, whether they are Twitter users or not. Consider everything you ever tweet to be on permanent record. Be judicious. Remember that every tweet appears in the feed of those following you. If you keep banging the same drum, they will cut you loose. Use your twitter powers wisely.

Facebook Pages

For the reasons I mentioned above, I don't think it's a great idea to direct readers to your personal Facebook profile. Aside from that, there are some very powerful things you can do with a Facebook Page that you can't do with a normal profile.

I've just set mine up (as a result it's not very pretty or exciting at the moment, but it will be) and I am still exploring all of the possibilities. If you want to check out what you can do with this tool, this is the definitive article: www.techipedia.com/2011/build-facebook-page/

Making Friends Is Nice but...

...what's the overall strategy? My aim is to create as many ways for people to find information about me or my work as possible. I look at all of these tools as an interconnected little world. My book listing on Amazon connects to my Author

Page, which in turn links to my blog and my Twitter feed. My Facebook Page has links to my Twitter feed, my blog, and my book listings on Amazon. My blog has links to my books, my website, my Twitter feed... you get the idea.

A reader now has a number of ways to discover my writing, and a number of different ways to engage with me if they choose. They might prefer Twitter, they might like to read my blog, they might like to interact on Facebook, they may choose to start a conversation on Goodreads, LinkedIn, LibraryThing, or Shelfari.

The point is, by using as many different strategies as possible, you are giving the reader vastly increased opportunity to find you and engage with you, and an engaged reader is far more likely to buy your book and your subsequent books.

This is the most important part: an engaged reader is an invested reader. They are interacting with you because they enjoy it, and, because they enjoy it, they want you to succeed. They will tell their friends about your books and some of those will tell their friends, and so on. *Ad infinitum.*

Of course, all of these strategies will mean nothing if you don't have a good story. Do not get too distracted by social media because the best marketing tool, the most powerful promotional weapon a writer has, is new work. I can't repeat this enough. Your writing time should be sacrosanct. Only spend time on marketing and promotion when you have hit your writing targets or when you can't write for whatever reason. The only time I make an exception to this is around the time of a new release. Other than that, nothing gets in the way of writing. Be disciplined.

Step 8: Reviews

Some people are skeptical about the power of reviews and whether they have any significant impact on sales. However, I think this is a very short-sighted view. While readers may ignore a book with just a couple of positive reviews, assuming the reviews have been left by the author's mother or lover (or, in some cases, the author themselves), there is no doubt that 50 overwhelmingly positive reviews will help sales.

Instead of weighing the possible effect of one positive review, you have to start looking long-term and considering how to obtain lots of positive reviews. If you are serious about making a career out of writing, you have to take your nose out of the day-to-day. Stop looking at each little bump and dip in your rankings and trying to divine reasons for each. Instead, start planning for the future.

Reviews should be part of the marketing plan for every writer.

Paid Reviews

A number of venues out there allow an author to pay for a review. Some are respectable; some are not. Either way, I think paying for a review is a huge mistake. There are a multitude of places where you can submit your book for genuine review for free—even self-published works—and these are where you should focus your energy.

People justifiably question the integrity of a paid review, so it should be obvious why going down this road is a mistake. In short, if you are thinking about paying for a review, don't.

Amazon Reviews

Anyone can leave a review on Amazon, whether they have bought the product or not, which has led to abuses in the past and left some customers mistrusting reviews—especially when an author's only two glowing reviews are both from people who have reviewed nothing else.

To avoid getting tarred with the "fake review" brush, I recommend that you ask your friends *not* to post reviews. If they insist, there's not much you can do about it, just ensure they know their review must be genuine or it could harm your reputation. Readers are savvy, and false reviews can be spotted a mile away.

To avoid getting lumped in with the sock-puppets, you want to move past having just one or two reviews as quickly as possible. One simple way is to offer a limited number of free copies for review on a forum such as Kindle Boards.

(Note that reviews from Amazon US don't get posted to Amazon UK, and vice versa, unless the reviewer does it manually. Consider Kindle Users Forum for finding UK reviewers.) Make your announcement enticing and do it in the appropriate place (there are strict rules). Remember, even in giving your book away for free you are asking people to donate their most valuable resource: time. Never forget they are doing *you* a favor, and act appropriately.

Start by limiting the amount of review copies to five. This makes it seem exclusive and not as if you are just handing out unlimited copies to anyone willing to say something nice. You can also host a giveaway on your site, which can be great for generating interest, and ask winners to leave a review if they enjoyed the book. Those who lose may decide to buy the book anyway (and review it).

When someone expresses interest in reviewing your book, there are a number of ways of providing a review copy.

You can simply e-mail the file to the reviewer, which is the simplest way and costs you nothing, although some worry about piracy in doing so. (I don't. I believe obscurity is a far greater threat!)

Alternatively, you can go to your listing on Amazon and beneath the button to purchase there is a button to "Give as a Gift." Problem is, you have to pay full price for this, including any applicable VAT/sales tax.

If you choose this option, it will count as a sale, and you will receive royalties. Essentially, it costs you the price of the book minus the royalty you receive. I do this sparingly for a number of reasons. It artificially inflates your sales figures, giving you a false picture of how your e-book is selling and making it difficult to track genuine sales because it doesn't add to your figures right away, only when the receiver actually accepts the gift (which could be days or weeks later). Also, the person you give a copy to doesn't actually have to redeem it for your book; they can purchase something else if they like. I believe this happened with a couple of copies I gave to reviewers—it's quite common, and there's nothing you can do about it so there's no point getting worked up about it. Finally, you pay for it, so it's not a sustainable sales strategy!

However, giving your work as a gift through Amazon is useful in very limited circumstances. If there is someone you want to impress, for example, it looks far better to get a fancy e-mail from Amazon than just an attachment by e-mail.

A third way is to use a Smashwords coupon, which is probably the best of all. Your Smashwords account allows you to generate a coupon giving someone a percentage off your book's price. You can set this percentage to 100%, giving them a free copy. The advantage in doing so is that it looks good, the piracy worries (if you have them) are lessened, and the reviewer is then encouraged to review on Smashwords too (Smashwords allows reviews only from those who purchased on their site), as well as Amazon (which doesn't have such requirements).

The only drawback with the Smashwords coupon is that the reviewer might inadvertently just post their review there, and not on Amazon, which is where you really want it. Also, you should make sure all the peculiar Smashwords formatting quirks are removed from your book before you send coupons to reviewers.

Overall, if you are only giving five or ten Amazon copies away for review, that's fine. If you are going beyond that, or are doing a large giveaway, stick to Smashwords coupons. If the only sales you can get are from buying copies of your book yourself, you're not going to be in this game very long.

In time, the reviewer will (hopefully) post the review. Don't chase them, which will only annoy them. Remember, they are doing *you* a favor. Also, a reviewer may have decided not to review your book because they didn't like it—another reason not to push them.

Book Blogs

Book review sites have become popular ways for readers to find books, especially e-books. Getting mentioned on some of the most popular blogs can have a huge positive effect on sales. Amanda Hocking said one of the factors in her success was getting to know the book bloggers and getting plenty of reviews for her books. There are so many sites that it can seem daunting at first, but a few handy lists out there break them down by genre.

Check the submission guidelines and follow them to the letter. Be professional in your approach. Tailor each e-mail. Address it personally to the reviewer and make it brief while still providing all the information they require. Most bloggers only select books that interest them, so make sure you describe yours in an enticing way to make it sound like something they want to read. Their guidelines will tell you how they prefer to receive the book. I've found that very few want it "gifted" on Amazon, or even a Smashwords coupon; usually, they just request you e-mail them the file.

Be warned that some of the most popular sites have waiting lists of six months or more. Get in line. There's a reason these reviewers are popular: their blogs have lots of readers. Wait your turn, e-books aren't going anywhere and don't have a shelf life. If you're lucky, sometimes your description will catch the reviewer's eye and you may skip the queue. Other sites are closed for submission altogether. Bookmark such sites and check back (or follow them on Twitter).

How to Deal with Reviews

Everyone gets the occasional bad review. Everyone. You just have to suck it up. The first time it happens, it will piss you off. Get over it. If someone paid money for your story, they have every right to tell others they thought it sucked. Even if it was someone you gave a free copy to and they didn't like it, you wasted their time so they have a right to express their view.

You may be tempted to respond, especially if there is something incorrect or unfair in their review. Don't. This can lead to an internet pile-on you can only imagine. In any event, remember that while a good story might please everyone, a *great* story tends to divide people. If you suspect you are being targeted unfairly and people who haven't even read your book are leaving reviews (this sometimes happens), you can contact Amazon and ask them to remove a review.

Some people may disagree, but I think an author shouldn't directly respond to a positive review either. My reasoning is this: there are plenty of trolls out there who just love to cause trouble. If they see an author who responds to reviews, they may leave a stinky one-star just to get a reaction. Don't play into their hands. Besides, if you have a few positive reviews and a couple of negative ones, but you have only responded to the positive ones, it will look self-serving. Don't do it. In any event, there is nothing like a handful of negative reviews to lend authenticity to the rest of your (hopefully overwhelmingly positive) reviews.

The only time you should respond to a positive review is when it comes from a book blogger. In this case, a simple thank you by e-mail, Twitter, or in the comments section of their blog is appropriate, but keep it brief. It's also no harm to tell them you have something else coming out soon—you could skip the queue that way.

When you get a nice review from a book blogger, tell the world. Put a link to the review on your blog, tweet the link, and put it on your Facebook page telling people to check it out. Book bloggers appreciate that, and it's good for you too. It's far better to send out "news" like this about your book than to tweet the Amazon link to your book every few days. It's less spammy and far more effective.

Following these simple steps, I picked up over 100 reviews in 2 months, spread across Amazon, Goodreads, LibraryThing, Smashwords, and book blogs.

In the *Resources* section of this book I've included links to several lists containing hundreds of book bloggers. Most of these lists are broken down by genre, and you should target reviewers accordingly. Once you get a review, determine whether there is something you can use in your book's promotional material, especially your book description. A juicy quote can add a lot of weight to your blurb.

Reviews are just another part of the puzzle—another way to jump-start word-of-mouth. Don't panic if you don't see a rise in sales straight away. You are building something bigger, remember that.

Step 9: Competitions, Discounts, Giveaways and Blog Tours

The final steps of this self-publishing guide are going to focus on further marketing tips. We have already covered the basics: blogging and websites, pricing, social networking, and reviews. Now, I want to talk about discounts, competitions, giveaways, and blog tours.

Discounts

Discounts can be a powerful incentive for readers to take a chance on your work. In your Smashwords Dashboard (one of the tabs at the top), you will see a menu on the left where you can generate coupons. You can set the amount of the discount in percentage terms (or choose a set discounted price), and you can time limit the coupon.

In terms of promotion, coupons are gold. Readers love them and you can tie them into all sorts of things. Consider giving a guest blog (more on that later) and allowing readers to buy your book at 25% or even 50% off for the following week.

Why not do something similar for your own blog readers as a "thank you" when you release a new title? After all, these are the people you need to help promote your book. Also, you can offer 20% off during slow periods, such as holiday weekends or summer months, or blast Twitter with a one-day only offer to breathe life into flagging sales.

There are so many possibilities. Just be aware that discounting will not work with 99c titles. Any discounts must remain above Smashwords' minimum price of 99c. However, you can still generate a free coupon, which is handy for review copies, competitions and giveaways. But don't forget to time limit the coupon. Coupons are multiple use and you don't necessarily want a free coupon that never expires out there in the public domain.

Competitions and Giveaways

Giveaways can be useful promotional tools and can help you attract a bunch of new readers, who may go on to review your book and spread the word. However, if you do giveaways too often, they can devalue your work. I talked about how to use giveaways to garner reviews in *Step 8*.

There are an infinite number of ways you can run competitions—you are only really limited by your imagination (and as a writer you should have that in spades). When setting up a competition, you need to be clear about your goals. Do you want more Twitter followers, more fans on your Facebook page, more blog views or subscribers, more word-of-mouth, more reviews, or do you simply want to sell more books?

These are all valid goals, and, if you are lucky, you can target more than one with a good competition. However, you should decide what your primary goal is, and tweak your competition accordingly. You do *that* by modifying the mode of entry. You might have people enter the competition by sending a tweet, posting to your Facebook Page, becoming a follower, or subscribing to your blog.

A free copy of your book is a suitable prize that costs you nothing (unless you "gift" it through Amazon), after all that is what you are trying to promote. Some writers use special prizes, such as Amazon gift cards or even Kindles, to increase interest. While this can attract a lot of attention, I wouldn't recommend it until you have a substantial social media following. It's a significant expense, and as always you should measure expected results against how many book sales you have to make to cover the cost of the prize.

As for timing, I've always gone with a few days after my book's release. That way, I don't cannibalize my opening-day sales, and I can use the competition to keep up momentum.

Here are some guidelines I suggest for a successful competition:

1. Use your blog. I post on the day of the competition, giving details on how to enter, what the prize is, and when the draw will take place. You can also use your website, a forum post, Facebook, or even Twitter. Personally, I think your blog is best. You can use all of the others to point towards your blog post.

2. Keep it simple. Too many competitions get complicated. If you require readers to follow your blog, tweet something, then post in the comments, then click "like" on Facebook—it will all be too much and you'll get fewer entrants. By all means, encourage entrants to spread the word by providing spot prizes or extra "entries" in the draw, but keep the actual entry simple or most people won't bother.

3. Tell people. No-one is going to enter if they don't know about it. Post details to Facebook, Twitter, forums, and the like, and tweet about it several times throughout the day.

4. Entice people. Make the prize sound interesting, whatever it is. Even if it is only a free e-book that costs you nothing, talk it up. Make people want it.

5. Consider running it on a Friday. Let's face it, people are in a better mood on Fridays. I have received a significantly better response from promo activities, especially on Twitter, on Fridays.

6. Make it fun. People are far more likely to spread a message if it's funny or interesting. A standard, boring promotional link is unlikely to spread.

7. Go viral. For maximum effect, you want your message to go beyond your immediate circle of followers. To do that you need to think about what you are including in your message. I ran two competitions in May 2011. The first had a great message for people to tweet (always give them the tweet to make it as easy as possible for people to enter). Mine was:

I want a #free #kindle copy of IF YOU GO INTO THE WOODS by David Gaughran so bad that it hurts http://amzn.to/mueQgC

That tweet has several important elements—my book title, hashtags to increase visibility, and a shortened link that takes people to the book page on Amazon—and it's fun, so people like to spread it. I got a great response to that competition and a lot of reviews from the winners.

Unfortunately, I made a major mistake. I originally included the link to my Amazon UK page, sending more than 70 US readers to the wrong page. By the time I realized, it was too late. That was a killer and I lost a lot of potential sales. Lesson learned—the hard way. Always double-check your links. Once something is on Twitter, you can't change it. Even if you delete the tweet, that original tweet can still be retweeted endlessly.

For the second, I tried something a little different. The tweet wasn't as fun, but the link went straight back to the competition in an attempt to expand its reach by increasing the number of entrants.

#Transfection Spreads Across The Planet! http://bit.ly/fection

With this approach, I actually had more sales during the competition, but the blog traffic was less than half. It's clear to me that the first approach is better and, if I had included the correct link, it would have beaten the second competition on all metrics by far.

These ideas should be a starting point for you. I'm sure

you can come up with something better if you put a little thought into it. If you can tie a competition in with the theme of your book somehow, that's best of all. The key is to try to be creative and encourage your entrants to be creative too. Allow multiple entries and bonus prizes for extra promotional efforts undertaken by entrants. If they start promoting the competition themselves, you are expanding your reach beyond your usual audience without any extra work on your part.

Blog Tours

A blog tour is essentially a scheduled series of guest blog appearances designed to mimic a book tour. You get the chance to introduce yourself and your work to new audiences. The blog host gets some free content and potential new readers following you over, and you aim to get some sales and to have some people follow you back to your blog.

There are companies you can pay to organize a blog tour on your behalf, but—like so many author promotional tools—I feel there are innumerable free possibilities you should explore first. If you insist on paying for a blog tour, as always, estimate whether it is worthwhile by weighing up the cost in the number of books you would have to sell to cover it.

A free approach can have great results. I am currently on The Never-Ending Blog Tour. A lot of people have asked me what this entails and how I set it up. It couldn't be simpler. I wrote a blog post asking whether any bloggers out there would like a day off. I cross-posted the question on a few forums and that simple approach got me more guest spots than I had time for—and it didn't cost me a dime.

After you have done a few guest blogs, other bloggers may contact you too. Give the host a couple of different ideas for guest posts and let them decide, because they know their readers best. Make sure you give them something original, not just something copied from your blog or that you have used before.

Have a look around at other writers' blogs; often they do interviews or feature indie books. Send them an e-mail—most people are very approachable—then schedule a time for the guest post, and turn it in ahead of time.

Make it easy for them. They are doing *you* a favor. I think it's always good form to offer to answer any questions that arise in the comments, and then drop back later to check. You should also cross-promote the guest post on your blog to send your host blogger as many readers as possible.

Don't be shy about promoting your books, but don't be obnoxious about it either. Talking about how you came up with the idea, or the excitement you felt on releasing it, or how to get reviews, is far more effective than asking people to buy your book.

As always, try to think like a reader. What are they interested in? Maybe they want to know a little more about the characters or the world you have built, or maybe they want to hear more about how you choose a book cover. Reading the blog you are to appear on will give you a sense of what the audience is interested in, and you can tweak your piece accordingly.

Hosting people on your blog can be a good idea too. Not only do you get a day off but you can get new readers, and maybe some sales out of it. But, like most promotional activities, the results aren't always tangible or immediate.

As you will read in *Part Three*, success in self-publishing is almost always a slow build. Sometimes readers need to hear about your books a few times before they buy. Keep getting your name out there, but, most importantly, keep writing.

Step 10: What Happens When Your Sales Just Stop?

All self-publishers experience a dip in sales at some point. Many will also experience a run where they sell nothing at all. It happened to me just after my second release. My sales just died—three days after a new release!

I sold none of either title in the UK for a week, and I sold nothing in the US for four days. Then, just as suddenly, sales picked up again. This happens. Sometimes it's a reporting delay by Amazon, but usually it's because nobody is buying your books.

There is one thing that is guaranteed *not* to increase your sales: checking your KDP reports every fifteen minutes. That's one thing you've got to nip in the bud right from the start. Self-publishers have all sorts of information at their fingertips, which is both a blessing and a curse. It is great to have up-to-date figures so you can, say, track the initial sales burst of a new release and, once that begins to fade, roll out a competition, but some people find checking reports addictive.

It's a complete waste of time, but I understand the temptation. What you need to do is set a time each day for checking your figures, and then forget about them outside of that. I check mine in the morning, and again before I go to bed so I can update my records.

The only time I might check it outside of that is if I see unusual amounts of traffic going from my blog to my Amazon listings. I might then look at sales figures to ascertain whether a certain post is bringing new visitors to check out my work.

But what do you do when your sales just stop? For starters, don't panic. Very few people have consistent sales numbers (at any level), and this is especially true when you are starting out. Some days are just better than others. Sometimes you have nothing for a while, and sometimes you get an inexplicable flurry. Some weeks are better than others.

The first thing you need to do is analyze whether it is just a random dip or whether it is a slump. If your book has been selling well but has a bad few days, ignore it. By all means, get it out of your system: bitch and moan, pour yourself a whiskey, take the dog for a walk, whatever it is you need to do, do it, then move on. Worrying about it won't help, and wallowing in it won't help either.

However, if you are seeing sales drop week-on-week (or they never happened in the first place), you might need to take a closer look. First, isolate all of the factors that are outside of your control. My sales halved in June 2011. That could have been worrying, but it wasn't. I knew from talking to lots of other self-publishers that their sales were down too.

In summer, when the weather is great, people spend more time outdoors. They are less likely to be reading e-books. On top of that, Amazon ran a promotion discounting 600 popular books from large publishers. They even put a button on everyone's listings drawing attention to these bargains. The sale was powerful enough to knock all of John Locke's books out of the Top 100, have an impact on Amanda Hocking's rankings, and cut Joe Konrath's sales by 15%. If those guys were going to get hurt by such a stunt, it's no surprise it was killing my sales.

I could have been annoyed about it, especially because the sale ad was more visible than my "buy" button, but I had to look at the bigger picture. Cheaper bestsellers will encourage more readers to make the switch to reading e-books. It might hurt me in the short-term, but long-term the pie will grow quicker. Also, there was nothing I could do about it except ride it out. Sure enough, as soon the sale ended things picked up again.

What if you have isolated all of the factors outside your control and you are still experiencing a sales slump? What if it's December and everyone else's sales are taking off? In that case, you need to look at your whole package to see where you can make improvements—and you can always make improvements. What you need to do is look at every aspect of what you are presenting to see how you can make it better.

Your Cover

Be honest with yourself, do you have a great cover? Maybe you rushed the release, maybe you didn't want to (or couldn't afford to) splash out for a professional. Look at the books at the top of the charts. Is your cover that good? *Really?*

A good cover is the third most important factor in a reader's decision to buy a book. The first is having read something by the author before and enjoyed it, and the second is a recommendation from a trusted source. Cover design is the only one of those three factors that is in your direct, immediate control. For a new writer, having an excellent cover is especially important.

Look at yours and see if you can make it better (and don't forget, you can have a great cover but still fall down if it doesn't give your readers the right impression of your work). Is the cover related to the book's content? Maybe you have written a romance, but the cover looks more literary. Maybe you have an illustrated cover that screams YA when your book is really for adults. Consider your cover design carefully.

Your Blurb

Did you spend enough time writing enticing copy for your blurb? Read your blurb as a stranger would. Does it draw you in? Can you make it better? Be harsh on yourself. A good blurb should be exciting and must make the reader really want to read the book. Every sentence should build towards that goal. If there is a sentence in there that doesn't sell your story, rewrite it or cut it.

If you have had nice reviews from book bloggers, take a quote or two from the review and put it in the blurb as a "testimonial." Again, look at the bestsellers and take note of the good blurbs, then copy what they do.

Your Sample

Most readers sample the writing before purchasing an e-book. Download your own sample and look at every aspect of it. Is the formatting perfect? Do your title page and copyright notice look professional? Does it look exactly like a best-selling book from a New York or London publisher? If not, fix it.

The first impression you give the reader is crucial. Most purchasing decisions are made on the strength of the sample. Make sure you have an enticing opening—it doesn't have to be explosive, but it must draw a reader in. You have limited space to grab a reader's attention, especially with short stories.

How large is your sample? If readers are wading through contents pages, prefaces, forewords, and dedications to get to the start of the story, they will get very little of your actual book to read. In fact, you might even lose them before they get to the opening. Can all of the "front matter" be moved to the back so the reader is thrust into the story as soon as possible? A great opening that will really grab people shouldn't be buried under pages of stuff a reader doesn't care about.

Those who do purchase your e-book can access the table of contents at the touch of a button. Put that, and anything else that is cluttering up your opening, at the back. Condense the title page and copyright notice into one page, so readers get straight into your story. Sample space is valuable so you should give readers as much of the actual book as possible in order to hook them.

Pricing

Have you tried experimenting with an alternative pricing strategy? I covered the basic options in *Step 5*, but is your pricing strategy aligned with your goals? Have you given it enough time to be able to assess it properly? If you have, and it's still not working for you, consider changing it. Each book has its own sweet spot—find yours.

A well-promoted sale can have great results. Advertise the drop in price and mention that it is time-limited. Readers who were sitting on the fence about purchasing your work might turn into impulse buyers. Sometimes you may need to raise the price. There is a glut of novels priced at 99c, so perhaps you could try $2.99. Don't be afraid to experiment.

Promotion

If your cover, blurb, and sample are all in great shape, and you are happy with your pricing, then you may need to look at what you are doing in terms of promotion. After all, the best package, combined with the best writing, will do nothing for you if nobody knows about it.

I have already elaborated on the importance of blogging and websites, social networking, and reviews, as well as discounts, competitions, giveaways, and blog tours. Have you explored every aspect and found what works for you? Is there something new you could try?

Ask for Help

Don't be afraid to seek advice. Ask people for an honest opinion of your entire book package and listen to what they have to say. There are plenty of forums out there where self-publishers hang out and other self-publishers usually take the time to help. Kindle Boards is particularly useful. Forums are also a great source of marketing ideas because pretty much everything has been tried by somebody at least once. Ask around.

Sometimes we can't see the flaws in our own product or strategy, and it takes a dispassionate stranger to point them out. Once pointed out, the problems usually seem obvious, but only if you're open to criticism. Divorce yourself from the work and remove the emotion, it's the only way you can even begin to be objective.

Don't Panic!

Keep your wallet in your pocket. There are a growing amount of paid services available to writers, most of which come with a string of glittering promises but aren't actually worth the money.

There aren't enough hours in the day to do all of the free promotional things you could try. If you are tempted to pay for an ad or a blog tour, ask yourself one simple question: how many sales will it bring in? A $100 blog ad is 300 sales of a 99c book. Do you really think the ad will boost your sales *that* much? Have *you* ever bought a book because of an ad?

You might hear people say that an ad gave them a significant bump in sales, and there are a couple of sites that can give results, such as Pixel of Ink or Kindle Nation Daily. However, ads on these sites tend to be booked months in advance. Most other sites simply don't get the traffic from readers or have the promotional set-up to give a similar boost. In any event, the best results are often achieved by writers who have already built up a substantial audience, which means an ad may not do as much for someone just starting out. My advice: keep your money.

And, whatever you do, never pay for a review. It's unethical, it's dumb, and it's a waste of money.

The Most Powerful Promotional Tool

You never know when your promotional efforts are going to bear fruit. There is an old adage that half the money you spend on advertising is wasted but the problem is you never know which half. I think the percentage of social media that is effective is more like 10%.

I see it as being like a farmer scattering a mystery bag of seeds in an open field. You don't know which ones will take and which will be eaten by birds, and you never know when they might blossom. This game is about patience and luck as much as it is about hard work and talent. Don't be disenchanted if your sales are slow to take off, or if you have a dip. Remember, the one activity guaranteed not to increase your sales is constantly checking your sales.

Keep getting the word out, and keep submitting to book bloggers, but, most importantly, keep writing. Even for John Grisham, Stephenie Meyer, or Amanda Hocking, the most powerful promotional tool is new work. Nothing gives sales of your existing work a bump like a new release. It's no accident that the majority of successful indie writers have a string of titles. Each book increases your virtual shelf space. Each one is another way for readers to find you. Each release is accompanied by promotional efforts that leave "breadcrumbs" all over the internet and lead readers back to you and the rest of your books.

It takes time to build an audience. It takes time for you to find your readers. Sometimes it takes several books. If you really want to give your sales a shot in the arm, stop worrying about it, and get back to writing. It's your job after all.

PART THREE: SUCCESS STORIES

The media likes to report on only the three most prominent self-published authors: Hocking, Konrath, and Locke. However, a large group of writers have made a success out of digital self-publishing. Some are selling in numbers to rival those three, and others have just started out but are already selling more than a thousand books a month. Thirty-three of them were kind enough to share their success stories with me in their own words.

1. Cheryl Shireman

I published my first novel, *Life Is But A Dream*, a little over four months ago. Since then, it has sold thousands of copies. Thousands! So far, sales for every month have more than doubled the sales for the previous month. I am astounded and very grateful. As sales increase, other writers are asking me for tips. They want to know my secret to success. I guess I could sum it up in one word: perseverance.

I started writing at the age of 13 and never stopped. I married shortly after high school, had three children, and went through a heart-breaking divorce. And continued writing.

I enrolled in college at the age of 28. I was working full-time in a factory and one afternoon as I was driving to work I passed my kids coming home in their school bus. Right then and there, I decided to go to college. With a degree, I could get a "day job" and be home with my kids at night. That was my motivation. So I applied.

Up to that point the only college textbooks I had ever read were the ones I bought at Goodwill for 25c. They were old, dusty anthologies of American and English literature that I took home and studied after the kids were asleep. I highlighted and underlined the words of Steinbeck, Cather, Wordsworth, and Poe. Secretly, I was envious of the people who actually took such classes and read such books.

Much to my surprise, I was not only accepted but excelled in my classes. I loved the writing and literature classes. I remember one tough semester when I had to read 33 novels. I was ecstatic. In those writing classes, I began to hone my skill. I also started submitting novels (some really awful and some just bad) to publishing houses and collecting rejection slips. And I continued writing.

I remarried, completed my undergraduate degree with a major in Creative Writing and American Literature, and eventually enrolled in graduate school. And I continued writing. A couple of my books gained some agent interest, and I even came very close to a publishing contract. Close, but no cigar. I completed graduate school and served as a ghostwriter for two non-fiction books that were published for a major publisher. And I continued to write.

Then, for Christmas 2010, my husband bought me a Kindle. I didn't want it. In fact, I was angry when I opened the present. I wanted nothing to do with reading a book on an electronic device. I love books—the look of them, the smell of fresh ink, and even the way they feel in my hands. But in less than a month I had over 100 books on that unwanted Kindle.

In late January of 2011, I was browsing Amazon and came across a book by Karen McQuestion. I read she had published several of her novels directly through Amazon. I started researching this possibility immediately. There had to be a catch. It seemed too good to be true. There was not. Within 48 hours of reading that small blurb about McQuestion, I submitted my recently completed novel *Life Is But A Dream* (a novel I sporadically worked on for 10 years). Within another 24 hours it was available for the Kindle. Within another couple of weeks it was also available for the Nook and as a paperback through Amazon. The cost of all of this was less than $10 to ship a "proof" copy of the paperback. I wondered if I would sell a single copy.

Now, thousands of sales later, it is all a bit overwhelming because even though I have been writing for years, these last four months have felt like a whirlwind. I am so grateful for my readers (they are literally making my life-long dream come true), and for my husband, because if it were not for that unwanted Kindle, right now I would probably be going through the very time-consuming pattern of submission to multiple agents and publishers. Instead, I am writing another novel.

I am convinced the only difference between a successful writer and an unsuccessful writer is perseverance. If you dream of being a writer, do it. It is within your power. Write. Read books in your genre, but read the classics too. Take as many classes in writing as you can afford. If at all possible, get a degree. Better yet, a graduate degree. And write. Always write.

Amazon: amzn.to/iMswKd
Website: cherylshireman.com
Twitter: twitter.com/cherylshireman
Facebook: facebook.com/cherylshireman

2. Victorine Lieske

My publishing journey started in April of 2010 when I uploaded my book *Not What She Seems* to the Kindle. I really had no expectations. I had tried selling the e-book on Lulu and had sold three copies in six months, two to friends. My first month on Kindle I sold seven copies. I was thrilled with that!

I joined some forums where other authors were, I submitted my book to book reviewers, and I did some giveaways. By the end of June I had sold over 600 books. In July I raised my price to take advantage of the 70% royalty that Amazon was offering, which stalled my sales, but I wanted to leave it there for a while to see if I could market and get better results. After three months and sales slowing down, I decided to try lowering the price to 99c. That's when my sales took off.

By December I was selling several hundred copies a day. In February my sales peaked with an average of 1,000 sales a day across all sales channels. In March I made it on the *New York Time's* best-selling e-book list and stayed on the list for six weeks. I was stunned. I had never thought a self-published book would make it on the list. I began to get e-mails from agents wanting to know if I had representation. I signed with Rachel Vogel of Movable Type Literary Group.

I did get an offer for my second book, *The Overtaking*, but I declined it because I can earn higher royalties on my own. I have recently self-published that book as well and I'm beginning to market it. It's a YA romance, so I will need to tap into a slightly different audience.

Amazon: amzn.to/iIpGXO
Blog: victorinewrites.blogspot.com

3. Michael Hicks

I took the self-publishing route for the same reason many others do: because I couldn't win the lottery with the traditional publishing houses. When I finished my first book, *In Her Name* (omnibus edition) in 1994, there were only two options: traditional publishers or a vanity press. I wasn't interested in the latter for a lot of reasons, and after the usual round of rejection letters from publishers, I gave up writing and stuffed the box with the manuscript under my desk to use as a footrest for the next 14 years.

Enter the Amazon Kindle. We first learned about the Kindle in 2007. My wife and I bought a pair of the gadgets, and we loved them. Then I found out that you could publish books directly to the Kindle store. No agents or publishers required. Free. Easy (relatively speaking—the process was a bit rough around the edges then). Okay, heck—why not?

So, after a lot of work converting the *In Her Name* manuscript to digital form, I published it in 2008. For me, that was the accomplishment of one of my major life goals: to have a book published. It didn't matter that I was the one who'd done it. In fact, I thought that was pretty cool.

Much to my shock and delight, a few people bought the book. And they kept buying it. Then readers started to leave reviews saying they actually enjoyed it. The fact that I was making a bit of money from the whole thing was simply icing on the cake.

At that point, I had no professional aspirations for my writing. I considered my storytelling to be a hobby that happened to bring in some money without any real expense up front other than my time. I didn't spend much time trying to promote it beyond talking about it in a couple of web forums, but sales steadily grew until I was making a few hundred dollars per month in royalties.

Most importantly, though, publishing *In Her Name* got me back into writing. So after nearly fifteen years, I found myself back at the keyboard and working on my next novel, which turned out to be the first prequel, *In Her Name: First Contact*. Then came the next one, *Legend Of The Sword*.

I took a break at that point to try something different, a thriller called *Season Of The Harvest*. That was really the turning point, because I realized that this book had a lot of potential, and so I really started to work on promotion, mainly through Twitter.

The results have put me where I am today: five months after the release of *Season Of The Harvest*, I'm planning to resign from my 25-year career job to write full-time, because I can't afford not to. The work can be hard and the hours are long, but I love writing, and you love reading. If that's not a match made in heaven, what is?

Amazon: amzn.to/m2hNv7
Blog: authormichaelhicks.com
Facebook: facebook.com/authormichaelhicks
Twitter: twitter.com/KreelanWarrior

4. CJ Archer

I began self-publishing at the end of January 2011. I'd been reading Joe Konrath's blog and hearing about other success stories, but I wasn't convinced self-publishing was for me. After all, I didn't know the first thing about designing covers, formatting or marketing. But as the New Year rolled around I could see my dream of being published slipping further away.

I'd been agented for two years but my agent couldn't sell my square-peg books despite getting very close with one at a Big Six publishing house. All the rejections praised my writing and stories but mentioned the market was too tough, or romance readers weren't interested in paranormal historicals or books set outside Regency England. My Elizabethan-set books were just too different. I tried writing a more traditional romance, but it sucked. It just wasn't me. My agent and I parted company after that and I was on my own. The idea of starting from scratch again was overwhelming and I didn't want to do it. In fact, I no longer wanted to write.

So, instead of writing, I self-published those books. What did I have to lose? After all, the agent had loved my stories. Contest judges had loved them. I loved them and I thought they deserved a chance to see if readers did too. I spent the first four months re-reading those old manuscripts and preparing them for Kindle and Smashwords, one book at a time. Of these, *A Secret Life* was the historical romance that had crawled its way up the editorial ladder of the Big Six publisher only to be rejected at the top.

Lo and behold, I got some sales in the first days. Then

more sales came as I uploaded more books, including a 99c novella, *The Mercenary's Price,* which is my bestseller, averaging between 30 and 40 sales a day. I started getting fan mail asking about future books, and I received some fabulous four- and five-star reviews.

And I got paid. In May, just four full months after starting down the indie path, I sold more than 2,000 books and earned as much as I could in a part-time job. But best of all, I got my writing mojo back.

Amazon: amzn.to/mb7GeF
Blog: cjarcher.blogspot.com

5. Beth Orsoff

When I began self-publishing almost one year ago, I didn't know what to expect. I'd been seriously pursuing traditional publishing since 2001, and my first book *Romantically Challenged* had been published by Penguin/NAL in 2006. Unfortunately, my timing wasn't great. The chick-lit market crashed six months prior to the release of *Romantically Challenged*. Penguin gave it a small print run and no marketing support, and not surprisingly, the novel was not a bestseller.

I spent the next several years writing more humorous women's fiction (we weren't allowed to call it chick-lit anymore). Although these books were often praised by editors and loved by agents, they didn't sell.

Then, in early 2010, my world changed. I started reading Joe Konrath's blog and several of my friends and relatives purchased Kindles. One of them even sent me a link to an NPR interview with Karen McQuestion. Self-publishing was no longer for delusional hacks. Even good writers were self-publishing.

I discussed it with my agent, who was in the midst of shopping my most recent novel, *How I Learned To Love The Walrus* (An Arctic Romantic Comedy), to the major publishers. She thought it was a good idea to self-publish *Romantically Challenged* (the book was already out of print and the rights had reverted to me) just to "keep my name out there," but she didn't think I would sell many copies. And neither did my normally supportive husband. "But how will people find your book?" he asked, when I told him my plan. "I don't know," I replied. "How do you find a book in the book store?"

The first week *Romantically Challenged* was available on Amazon I sold four copies. I don't know how people found the book, but they did. Soon after, I discovered Kindle Boards and the Amazon forums and started connecting with other self-published authors. We commiserated when sales fell, cheered each other on when things were going well, and most importantly, we shared information. That, and old-fashioned trial and error, is how I learned the self-publishing ropes.

I uploaded my second novel, *Honeymoon For One*, a humorous cozy mystery, the month after I self-published *Romantically Challenged*. To my amazement, *Honeymoon For One*, which had never been traditionally published and didn't have the benefit of professional reviews, sold even better than *Romantically Challenged*.

Several months later I pulled *How I Learned To Love The Walrus* (An Arctic Romantic Comedy) from my agent and self-published that title too. Not coincidentally, that was the first month I sold over 1,000 books. And in less than a year I've sold more than 47,000 e-books.

Have I turned my back on traditional publishing? No. For the right offer I would still consider it. The difference is I'm no longer waiting around for the "right offer." I'm publishing my books on my own and loving it!

Amazon: amzn.to/iRlcly
Website: bethorsoff.com
Facebook: facebook.com/BethOrsoff

6. Bob Mayer

In the military it's a maxim that every army is always prepared to fight the last war, not the next one. That gets a lot of people killed. In the Green Berets we were always looking ahead, preparing for what would be, rather than what was. That was my Special Forces experience and I'm applying it to my writing career. Instead of looking at what *was*, I'm looking forward at what *will be*. That's the reason I've made the switch from traditional publishing to self-publishing.

My last three book deals with traditional publishers totaled over a million dollars, so I'm walking away from something significant. I've also hit all the bestseller lists—*New York Times*, *Wall Street Journal*, *Publishers Weekly*—but that doesn't equate directly to the bottom line.

My first book came out in 1991 and now, over 45 titles later, more than 4 million books sold, I'm more excited than I've ever been as a writer. Here's the thing authors need to understand: it isn't as much about what's happening NOW in publishing. It's where things are going to be a year from now.

There's a huge difference between an author promoting their book and a publisher tossing a book out there, because I have an incentive to promote and also know *how* to promote—something New York is still behind the curve on. I lead with the first book in the series at 99c. All of the rest of my fiction is priced at $2.99. I'm pricing *Duty, Honor, Country* at $4.99 because, at 175,000 words, it's epic (almost twice the length of my other books) and took me two years to write. Plus it includes 18,000 words from the opening of my next modern thriller, *The Jefferson Allegiance*. Follow-on books in the series will be priced lower, at $2.99, and come out faster, which is another key to success.

I don't think success is any easier in self-publishing. Both are very difficult. The main difference is that I have more control than I ever did in traditional publishing. Success will go to those who, first and always, have a well-written book with a great story. Then there is the need for persistence and consistency. While the digital age has made all this possible, I think it has the potential to make quitting much easier since we live in a time of instant gratification. Writers are checking their Kindle numbers daily and bemoaning lack of sales within a week of upload.

I think one trait those of us coming from traditional publishing have had is knowing it's the long haul that counts. Also, in digital, it's not the spike for the bestseller list, but the long tail of sales that is the key.

Amazon: amzn.to/ifYTue
Website: whodareswinspublishing.com

7. Debora Geary

Last Thanksgiving, while wandering aimlessly around the Internet, I discovered that writers could self-publish a book to the Kindle. As a lifelong avid reader and a devoted Kindle owner, this must have tripped some switch deep in my psyche—I woke up the next morning with the story idea that would morph into *A Modern Witch*. I started writing that evening, finished the first draft in under two months, and hit "publish" in the middle of March—less than four months after I learned such a thing was possible.

Now, three months after publishing, I am a week away from leaving my "day job" and becoming a full-time author. It's been a light-speed journey, with a lot of invaluable help along the way. The best part, however, is my readers. I get fan mail. Everyone, at least once in their lives, should be able to experience the blooming joy of an e-mail from a complete stranger saying that something you did matters. There's nothing like it.

My story is not all that typical—but it's possible, and that's an amazing thing.

Amazon: amzn.to/jILvIj
Website: deborageary.com

8. *Sibel Hodge*

A few years ago, after I wrote my debut romantic comedy novel *Fourteen Days Later*, I queried hundreds of agents and publishers. I got too many rejections to even count! OK, small white lie. A while ago (out of morbid curiosity) I did count them—it was a whopping two hundred!

I did come close to being traditionally published a couple of times, but it never quite worked out. It was either, "one group of editors liked it but another didn't," or "the chick-lit market is saturated," or "we love it but..."

When I first looked into publishing independently, platforms such as Amazon Kindle didn't support international authors. So the way I saw it, I had two choices: either I could write another book, hone my writing skills, learn all I could about my craft, and wait for an opportunity to come up, or I could let all the rejection letters get me down, think my writing career was over before it had begun, and stick my head in the oven!

Since heat tends to turn my curls into a ball of frizz, it was no contest, really. I wrote my next novel, a chick-lit mystery called *The Fashion Police*, and waited. Because I knew, I just knew, that I could do this. I could write novels that people wanted to read. If only I could get the chance.

In the meantime, I also entered several writing competitions. While I was still getting the dreaded rejections, *Fourteen Days Later* was shortlisted for the Harry Bowling Prize 2008 and received a "Highly Commended" from The Yeovil Literary Prize 2009. And *The Fashion Police* was a runner up in the Chapter One Promotions Novel Competition 2010 (and later nominated for the Best Novel with Romantic Elements 2010 by The Romance Reviews). Surely I was doing something right, wasn't I? But I *still* couldn't get a publisher!

Then last year, when Amazon opened up their doors to non-US authors, I uploaded *Fourteen Days Later* and *The Fashion Police* onto their Kindle store. I couldn't believe it when I finally saw my books on sale. It was scary, rewarding, exciting, amazing—so many experiences rolled into one.

But what if no-one liked my novels? What if I had all bad reviews? What if all the two hundred rejections were right? What if, what if…?

Time for a deep breath, Sibel. If you want to be an author, you have to repeat this mantra every day: "I can do this. I can do this. I *can* do this."

So I did.

And boy am I glad I did! The first month, with *Fourteen Days Later* and *The Fashion Police*, I sold 44 books (eek!). In January, I released my third novel, a romantic comedy called *My Perfect Wedding*, and in April I released my second chick-lit mystery *Be Careful What You Wish For*. In the past four months alone I've sold more than 25,000 e-books, and all my novels are consistently in the Amazon Top 100 genre categories for humor, contemporary romance, comedy, and romantic suspense. Considering there are over 950,000 Kindle books on Amazon, that's not bad!

But there is one lesson I've learned in the last couple of years: you can do anything you want to in life. It may mean you have to go a different route than the one you originally planned, but if you're determined enough and believe in yourself, you can overcome any obstacles.

So do you want your manuscript sitting unloved in a dusty drawer somewhere, or do you want readers? Thanks to the e-book revolution, the choice is now yours.

Amazon: amzn.to/j2MkoT
Website: sibelhodge.com

9. *Consuelo Saah Baehr*

A year ago I began to notice blogs about e-books. My son owned and loved his Kindle. I saw blogs about people who published almost anything—their dinner menu—for the Kindle, but many were whining about how hard it was to format the books for the new digital platforms. I hardly knew what digital meant and no-one knew HTML. I stayed on the couch.

One day I read about Nicholas Callaway, an apps creator who said, "all content was being re-imagined for entirely new platforms." I had lots of content that could be re-imagined and it was gathering dust on my bookshelves and my hard drive. Could I possibly participate in this? Could I repurpose my backlist books and my newly written books and be a repurposed writer? I got up off the couch.

I beseeched my brain to stay alert. I read the Smashwords Style Guide and began to format four novels, a memoir, a monologue, and a collection of short stories. I discovered a free program called Calibre that could convert files instantaneously. I hired my artist daughter to create new covers. When all was ready, we sat in my little office, pulled the upload trigger, and published the first title on Amazon. As Truman Capote said when he sold two short stories in one day, "Dizzy with happiness is no mere phrase."

It used to be that I would clean the oven to avoid writing because traditional publishing was total bleakness interrupted by 10 minutes of happiness when your agent called to say she had sold your book. There followed a year of silence while the book was "produced." Publication was brief. The salesmen (you heard right) decided the print run and if it was in the low five digits, the book was DOA. Two years of your life had been eaten up. The Prozac months followed. Now I write avidly because I can publish what I write. Once written and edited, I can publish a book in a matter of minutes and sell it 24/7. I have satisfied my two passions: writing and commerce. The commerce part required me to do some marketing work that is easily learned. I began a blog, started a Facebook page, bid for interviews and guest blogs, and generally made my brand visible. You can solicit reviews, but the best ones arrive unsolicited, left quietly by readers. The reader reviews for my e-book original *100 Open Houses* have been heartfelt and have helped me understand my own book.

For each of the first seven months in, sales doubled exponentially. In the eighth month, sales jumped dramatically, mainly due to re-pricing my title *Best Friends* to $0.99 and also having Amazon accept and market my monologue *Thinner Thighs In Thirty Years* in their Kindle Singles program. Now I'm in the 1000+ sales a month club.

Publishing e-books is the most liberating development to come along for authors in my lifetime. It's as monumental as the printing press. There is a serendipitous aspect to it that's exciting. Your book can take off for any reason. Suddenly there's a flurry of sales and you don't know why. It's just a marvelous flight into the inscrutable ether. The best part: the author is in control.

Amazon: amzn.to/mcOhi7
Blog: setthiswriterfree.blogspot.com/

10. Steven Hawk

My journey began a little over a year ago. I bought a Kindle in February 2010 and was immediately hooked on the e-book format. Through the course of my reading, I stumbled across some very good books written by indie authors and thought, "Hey, I can do this." I already had two manuscripts sitting in a drawer, and a few more in development, so content wasn't an issue. For me it was a question of "how" do I do this? I did some research and found a 99c e-book on Amazon by Edward Patterson called *Are You Still Submitting Your Work to a Traditional Publisher?* I credit Ed and his book with providing me with a road map for publishing on Kindle.

I published my first book, *Peace Warrior*, in July 2010. I sold 30 copies the first month and the numbers grew from there. December was my first month selling more than 1,000 books, and sales have grown each successive month since then. In April, I published the second book of the Peace Warrior Trilogy, called *Peace Army*. Putting out the second book really boosted sales. In May, I sold almost 4,000 copies of each book. So far, after 10 months of e-publishing, I've sold more than 20,000 books. I think when the third book is released later this year, the numbers will really skyrocket.

Ideally, I'd love to write full-time. If the numbers continue to grow, I can see that as a realistic possibility after the third book is released. I currently work about 50 hours a week at a full-time job that pays very well. It will be tough to leave that income, but I will let the numbers tell me what to do. Writing is something I do on a discretionary basis—usually an hour or so a couple of nights during the week and three to four hours each morning on the weekend. That limits me to a book every eight or nine months, at best. Working full-time, I think I could put out two books a year.

Amazon: amzn.to/jurcw6
Twitter: http:/twitter.com/stevenhawk
Facebook: facebook.com/steven.hawk1

11. Suzanne Tyrpak

I've had two agents, several of my short stories have been traditionally published, I've written numerous articles and press releases, and I've won a few awards. Most of the novels I've written are historical (suspense), set in ancient times. This, I've discovered, is a "tough-sell."

For example, a few years ago I attended a conference for historical fiction writers. An agent I encountered there refused to discuss my book because (her words): "No-one cares about Rome." I found her comment strange. At that time, HBO had just released the series Rome.

Eventually, I found another agent and my novel was shopped around. It received a lot of interest and came close to being published by Tor, but they were cutting back on historical novels. Another senior editor at Random House expressed interest, but Random House was letting go of senior editors at that time—he was one of them.

Then I went through a divorce. Finding time to write novels became a challenge. I began writing short stories— sharp and contemporary, very different from my novels.

Last summer, August 2010, my friend Blake Crouch suggested I publish for the Kindle. In August, I published nine short stories as a collection called *Dating My Vibrator (and other true fiction)*. Getting the stories out there has been wonderful. So wonderful that (with Blake's encouragement), I decided to do a rewrite on my novel *Vestal Virgin* and I self-published it as an e-book in December (also available as trade paperback). Now, both of my books are selling well.

Would I like to be traditionally published? Sure. But getting my work out and being read has been a great experience. I enjoy the writing community and the direct communication with writers and readers on forums like Kindle Boards. Self-publishing has opened up a whole new world and has put writing back into the hands of writers.

Ten months later, I've sold about 8,000 books—I'm currently selling about 50 books per day—and I expect that number to jump when I bring out my new collection of short stories this summer, *Ghost Plane and Other Disturbing Tales*. I plan to bring out another novel at the end of this year, *Agathon's Daughter—suspense in ancient Greece*.

I also expect to be supporting myself exclusively by writing at this time next year. I'm already close. But I'll probably keep my job at the airlines so I can fly around for free and get insurance.

I'd love to hear from you at my blog.

Amazon: amzn.to/m7zUkB
Blog: ghostplanestory.blogspot.com

12. Mel Comley

I began in October last year. Sales were very slow to start with but in January they really took off in both the USA and the UK. My thriller *Impeding Justice* reached #47 in the UK chart and #343 in the USA chart.

In May, I was contacted by several agents who had read my books and were interested in representing me. After mulling over the options and talking to several writers I've become friendly with on Kindle Boards, I decided to sign a contract with a top New York agent.

The one piece of advice I'd offer a writer starting out would be to employ a damn good editor. I'd also tell them that getting your work recognized is harder than you think. Writing the book is the easy part. The hard work starts when you have to promote it.

Amazon: amzn.to/kBYi0y
Amazon UK: amzn.to/iHzpb1
Smashwords: bit.ly/kcHFBL
Blog: melcomley.blogspot.com

13. Jason Letts

Writing used to be the bastard child of the arts, something lots of people did but only a couple could make a living from. Self-publishing in digital formats has changed all that, and I can personally attest to the way it has empowered writers to take control of their work and carry it as far as their visions and abilities can propel them.

I began writing young-adult fiction as a hobby while I was teaching English in Japan and published my first book on Amazon shortly before returning home to America. When I got back, the horrendous state of the job market made it my only source of income. It certainly wasn't enough to live on, but I continued to put time into my writing and promotion while I applied, in vain, for countless jobs.

As of today, my writing has become a much more lucrative source of income than any of those professional positions I applied for, earning me two or even three times their salaries. It pays all of my bills, funds my retirement account, and feeds my unquenchable hunger for travel. I'm extremely fortunate to hear from new readers who enjoy my work on a near-daily basis and have formed great connections with other writers you may read about in this collection. I'm doing what I love and continually pushing myself to do it better.

How did I go from earning extra pocket money to making it into the top 5% of indie writers? There were multiple factors. Self-publishing exposed me to the workings of the fiction market and gave me a better understanding of reader tastes, allowing me to channel my style and my stories to a larger audience. I saw what successful writers were doing, and I learned from them and worked with them, and we helped each other create new opportunities. Maybe most importantly, I embraced, rather than ignored, criticism and used it to improve. Writing fiction is about learning and getting better over time, not being certain your first novel is a work of unimpeachable genius.

To all of those writers who are thinking about what to do with their manuscripts, I recommend you think hard about your goals and what's going to get you there. No one path will ever lead two people to success, so you've got to find your own way and be creative while keeping your wits about you.

At the moment I'm working on a new YA dystopian novel entitled *Suspense*, which is due out in the fall. If you'd like to get in touch with me, you can find me on Facebook or my blog. Thanks for reading, and best wishes to you for the future!

Amazon: amzn.to/k7mqyG
Blog: powerlessbooks.com/blog/
Facebook: facebook.com/authorjasonletts

14. Melanie Nilles

I've been writing for nearly 19 years. In that time, I participated in writers' forums and workshops and even hired a great professional editor, all of which improved my writing (style, characterization, etc.). I've received plenty of rejection slips over the years.

My first acceptance came back in 2007, but after some difficulties with the publisher, I cancelled all but the one book they eventually published in 2008 (I had multiple books contracted). It doesn't say much when I was catching more mistakes than their editors were.

I've learned to take my time and have patience with the editing process since then, but a year after that first book I released my first self-published e-book, a novella that had been an Honorable Mention in the Writers of the Future Contest. After some editing on that, I put it out as a free PDF from my website and posted it at the minimum price on Amazon and Smashwords (which distributed it to other bookstores). That one, *A Turn of Curses*, was made free to all outlets earlier this year and when Amazon price-matched I saw it make it to the Top 100 free Kindle books in both the Amazon US and UK stores. I've seen a boost in sales of my other fantasy titles too, although

But I don't promote those books so much. I had made my *Legend of the White Dragon* books a free serial on my website, but it only saw a few hundred readers. I think having it free for a while helped attract a few of the right readers, who spread the word so that people started buying it when I made it available on Amazon, Barnes & Noble, and other sites through Smashwords.

The books I do the most work promoting are books in my *Starfire Angels* series. I first published *Starfire Angels* in 2009 and didn't do much promotion until the spring of 2010. In the last year, I've done just about everything a writer can do for those, including playing with price points. Sales climbed through January 2011 and have been good since.

A few weeks before releasing the third book of the *Starfire Angels: Dark Angel Chronicles* series, I made the first book, *Starfire Angels*, free everywhere. Once Amazon price-matched, it shot up to #18 on their Free Kindle books. It's since slipped down, but still sees a fair number of sales. It's helped sell the other books in the series by reaching a wider audience.

None of my individual books are priced higher than $2.99, and the fantasy omnibus, *Legend of the White Dragon: Legends, Legacies, Destiny*, is priced the same amount as the three individual books combined—$7.99—plus it includes appendices that are not included with the individual books.

Amazon: amzn.to/kNqvZO

15. Jan Hurst-Nicholson

Before being e-published, *But Can You Drink The Water?* went through a 25-year evolution, beginning as a stage script in the 1980s. After being advised that it would be more suitable for TV, I approached a local producer who asked for an outline of 13 episodes. But sadly it all came to naught when the SABC decided to drop freelance production. However, I still had the characters and situations wrestling to get out of my head, so I spent several months turning the episodes into a novel.

The manuscript trundled its way to various publishers (this was back in the days when you posted the complete script, at great expense, and were lucky to get a reply within three months). There were several, "we like it, however..." replies, one of which mentioned that the South African setting would work against it, so I turned three of the chapters into short stories and sold them to local and overseas magazines.

In 1993 I entered it in the Peter Pook humorous novel competition in the UK and it was a runner-up, but still no publishing contract.

In the meantime I was working on *The Breadwinners* (a family saga), *Leon Chameleon PI and the Case of the Missing Canary Eggs* (published by Gecko Books in 1993), *Leon Chameleon PI and the Case of the Kidnapped Mouse* (published in 1995), *Bheki and the Magic Light* (published by Penguin in 1996), and *Jake* (published by Cambridge University Press in 1999).

In 2002 I did yet another edit of *But Can You Drink The Water?* and sent it to another publisher, only to receive a reply saying, "if you had sent if five years ago we might have published it, but publishing is going through a difficult time and we have to be sure the book will be a commercial success." Back it went in the drawer.

In 2006 I took Richard Branson's advice of "screw it, let's do it" and published a compilation of my humorous articles, short stories (three of them taken from But Can You Drink The Water?) and other fun stuff as a paperback under the title *Something to Read on the Plane*. It has been selling steadily at airports in South Africa since.

In 2009 I put *But Can You Drink The Water?* on Authonomy, hoping to get a review by HarperCollins, but instead discovered the 2010 Amazon Breakthrough Novel Award. I entered and was thrilled to get to the semi-finals (Top 50 out of 5,000). The encouraging review from the *Publishers Weekly* judge prompted me to self-publish it as a Kindle e-book. I set the price at 99c (70p), believing readers wouldn't mind risking 99c on an unknown author or on trying an unfamiliar genre. Although sales began slowly, when Amazon UK came online they started to increase. So far I have sold in excess of 12,000 copies and it reached #20 in the top #100 bestseller list, and was #1 in three categories.

I have also e-published *Something to Read on the Plane, The Breadwinners, Mystery at Ocean Drive* (YA) and the *Leon Chameleon PI* series.

Amazon: amzn.to/jzZt7e
Website: just4kix.jimdo.com

16. KC May

The Kinshield Legacy was originally published by a small press. After about five years, I got the rights back and was deciding whether to shop it around to other publishers or put it out to pasture. Then it occurred to me that I could format it for e-readers like the Kindle and Nook and re-release it myself. I've really enjoyed the process and control of self-publishing. With the legacy publishing industry in flux, I decided not to spend years waiting to see if anyone would be interested in *The Venom of Vipers*. I self-published that one on December 1, 2010.

What I've learned is that if a book is good, readers will come. The more books you have available, the more likely you are to find an audience. It doesn't happen overnight, but with a little effort spent getting the word out, people will find you. Once they start talking about your book, it starts to snowball. Of course, my little snowball is still at the top of the hill, but it's gaining some momentum. I'm probably in the most exciting phase of the journey right now. :-)

Amazon: amzn.to/liitIF

17. Terri Reid

I was working as a consultant doing advertising, marketing and public relations for small to medium-sized local businesses when the economy crashed and my clients started tightening their belts and holding on to their money. Marketing budgets were slashed. My business was in trouble. I started looking for a full-time job, but there was nothing out there. Suddenly, the thought of writing for a living made sense, because, really, what did I have to lose?

I had been working on *Loose Ends* for months. I found myself with more time than money, so I worked nearly full-time to complete it. During that time, a friend sent me the *Wall Street Journal* article about Karen McQuestion and her amazing success in e-books. I had heard of Kindles, but I had no idea they held such a market share. Before I learned about Karen, I had planned to send my book off to an agent I was acquainted with in New York. But the biggest thing that sold me on e-publishing was the finances. I could get paid within 90 days of uploading my book. I could make the same amount of money on my e-book as I would through a traditional publisher. And my destiny was in my own hands.

I uploaded *Loose Ends* on August 3, 2010. I joined some forums and told them about my book. I went on Facebook and told my friends and family about my book and asked them to put my link on their Facebook pages. I called the editor of the local paper and told him about *Loose Ends* too. The paper did a Sunday feature about me and my book. (I had to borrow a Kindle from a friend for the photo.)

In August, I sold 142 copies of my book. In September, I sold 248 books. In October, I added another book, *The*

Ghosts of New Orleans. I had read that multiple books help you cross promote and should lead to more sales. *The Ghosts of New Orleans* was a novel I had written four years ago. It was a darker novel than The Mary O'Reilly stories, but I felt it still had merit. I did a quick edit and uploaded it on October 10, 2010.

In October, I sold 789 copies of *Loose Ends* and 195 copies of *The Ghosts of New Orleans.*

At the end of November, I added the second Mary O'Reilly book, *Good Tidings.* It was available on the night before Thanksgiving. By the end of the month, one week later, I had sold 142 copies of *Good Tidings,* 745 copies of *Loose Ends,* and 320 copies of *The Ghosts of New Orleans.*

In December, I watched my numbers climb and three weeks into the month found that both *Loose Ends* and *Good Tidings* had sold over 1,000 copies. By the end of December, I had sold more than 5,000 books. In March 2011, I uploaded *Never Forgotten,* the third book in the Mary O'Reilly series. I've been averaging 6,000 sales a month.

Now, the secret to my success is... there is no secret. I've heard rumblings that paranormal mysteries or paranormal romances are easy to sell. I didn't write my book because of market trends (although, really, that would have been brilliant.) I wrote it because that was the story I had to tell. I feel like I've been able to connect to my readers—I get e-mails almost every day from people who've read my stories and loved the characters.

What kind of advice can I share?

Write the very best story you can. Give it to someone else to edit. And then send it out there to find those people who have been waiting for your story.

Amazon: amzn.to/mSrC23
Facebook: on.fb.me/kTOzY3

18. Gerald Hawksley

I have been writing and illustrating books for very young children for more than 25 years now. That started out accidentally, but that is another story. How did I come to be publishing full-color children's picture books on a black and white e-reader, and furthermore, selling more than a thousand of them a month at $2.99?

It is hard to get a children's picture book published traditionally in the UK, and I wasn't getting anywhere. I was really relying on hack work from old contacts, and that was slowly drying up as they retired one-by-one. I toyed with the idea of self-publishing, and came across Amazon's Createspace print-on-demand service, but the figures didn't add up. I would have to sell my printed book for at least $12.99 to make a profit, and would be competing against trade paperbacks priced at $2.99.

Of course, I had heard of the Kindle, but had discounted it as a black and white e-reader only suitable for novels. I didn't even know it supported graphics at all. But I went and checked out the Kindle store and there were children's picture books on there after all. And then I noticed the free Kindle reading apps—Kindle for Mac, iPhone, Android, etc. I downloaded Kindle for Mac, and lo and behold, I could see full-color picture books on my Mac without even needing to buy a Kindle!

Traditionally published children's books don't really convert well to the Kindle, as they are usually created as double page spreads with integrated text. I thought if I could build a picture book especially designed to work on the Kindle, I might make a few sales. But, really, I did it as an experiment. I trawled through all my rejected manuscripts and half-formed ideas, and came up with *If You Have A Hat*, which I thought suited the format particularly well. I managed to cobble together a Kindle book and uploaded it. To be honest, I really wasn't expecting to actually sell any at all.

The first week I sold about a copy a day, which I thought was amazing. Then the numbers started slowly creeping up. I got a five-star review! Soon I was selling 20 a day. One day alone I sold 49 copies. Then I got a two-star review! Sales plummeted! But then slowly crept back up. Another five-star review! And now...

I have published three books since, but none has been as successful as *If You Have A Hat*. I didn't promote it at all; it just sort of started selling. Whether it will continue to sell, I don't know. Recently sales have been quite erratic. But, as an experiment, it was well worth trying.

Amazon: amzn.to/1Oi529

19. N Gemini Sasson

My journey into self-publishing came about after years of trying to break in via the traditional route. I had a wonderful, reputable New York agent who, beginning in 2005, submitted *The Bruce Trilogy* to publishers with relentless determination. We had a couple of near misses but in the end were unable to secure a contract. So I wrote another historical novel—a standalone that centered on a female character, which is what a few editors had said they were most interested in. By this time, however, the big slowdown in publishing was taking hold. A year later, we still hadn't had any luck, despite some very positive feedback. Both my agent and I were frustrated.

By then, I had writer friends who were self-publishing with POD paperbacks and through Kindle. My gut told me that was the way to go, so I talked it over with my agent and got his blessing. If nothing else, I figured I'd have something to show for all those years I wrote into a void with only hope to keep me typing away. I really didn't think I'd sell more than a few hundred books.

For the first six months, that turned out to be the case. With sales of just a few books a day, I signed up to take some college classes to renew my teaching certificate. But while I was sitting there in Anatomy class, something started to happen: sales began to snowball. Soon I was selling 10 a day on Kindle, then 20, then 50. Readers were sending e-mails asking when the final installment of the trilogy would be out and my book, *Isabeau, A Novel of Queen Isabella and Sir Roger Mortimer*, was regularly in the Top 100 Bestsellers in historical fiction on Kindle.

At my one year anniversary of self-publishing, I've sold more than 10,000 e-books. For now, I've shelved plans to look for a teaching job and am turning my full attention to writing. I am incredibly grateful my stories didn't have to be consigned to a desk drawer. Ten years ago, this wouldn't have been possible. While sales have far surpassed my original humble expectations, I realize success can be fleeting. I feel a pressure to keep writing, to get the next book out, but I also know that I can't rush it, because I don't want to disappoint loyal readers.

Although I still occasionally encounter the stigma self-publishers face, I no longer feel a need to defend it. Readers are the final validation. I try to keep my focus on that—that there are people out there reading what I've written and waiting for the next book. Traditional publishing certainly has its place, but it's also a business that can only take risks on so many new voices each year. Self-publishing takes work, patience and a lot of luck to succeed, but the rewards are tremendous. I truly feel that everything happens for a reason and this was meant to be my path into authorship.

Website: ngeminisasson.com
Amazon: amzn.to/kkwToV

20. Susanne O'Leary

When I published *Swedish for Beginners*, my first e-book, in February last year, my expectations were quite modest. In fact, I still remember the thrill I got at the very first sale. As the first e-book started to take off, selling some 100+ copies a month, I also uploaded some of the novels from my previously published backlist: *Fresh Powder* (a romantic comedy set in the Alps during a skiing holiday), and *Finding Margo* (contemporary fiction set in France). Sales started ticking away quite satisfactorily and the reviews came trickling in, most of them excellent.

I added four further titles during the year: *Villa Caramel* (a revamp of my earlier novel, *European Affairs*), *Silver Service* (a chick-lit romp set in Ireland), *A Woman's Place* (a historical novel based on a true story) and finally, my dip into the crime genre, a co-written murder mystery with the title *Virtual Strangers*.

All of last year these titles sold very well, meeting my expectations and more, and my US sales were twice those in the UK.

Just after Christmas I started to see a reversal of this trend; US sales slowed down and UK sales took off. By February I was selling twice as many e-books in the UK as the US and one of my books was nearly going viral. I was totally taken aback, both by the sales figures (now 100+ a day) and that this particular book was the one that would be the most popular—*Fresh Powder*, the "ski and socks" novel, about a group of people snowed into a luxury chalet in the French Alps, described in the Irish media as "Agatha Christie meets Mills & Boon on a James Bond set."

While I do think it's a fun novel and I thoroughly enjoyed writing it, I find it most peculiar that a seasonal winter story should still be selling in such numbers in June, staying in the Top 100 overall for more than a month. It has sold around 8,000 copies to date. I have no idea how or why this happened. I have done practically no promotion in the UK and it has only four reviews (all five stars). I can only surmise this occurred because of this mysterious thing called "word of mouth," which nobody knows how to manufacture. It's a huge lottery. But, like the old slogan says: "if you're not in, you can't win."

Website: susanne-oleary.com
Amazon US: amzn.to/mPKPGD
Amazon UK: amzn.to/ma08KZ

21. Mark Williams

Sugar & Spice was the first "indie" novel to break the legacy-published authors' stranglehold on the Kindle UK Top Ten.

Written by two previously unpublished writers under the search-engine friendly pen-name Saffina Desforges, *Sugar & Spice* was launched on Kindle after being rejected by almost every major UK agent. The book's length (120,000 words) and difficult subject matter (the hunt for a child-killer, which explores the innermost workings of the pedophile mind) resulted in comments like "unsellable" and "the last taboo," or "well written but no-one would buy it."

Undeterred, the Desforges partnership e-published on Kindle and continued to seek representation. One agent took the book under exclusive consideration and two months later, when the agency's reader gave a glowing review, asked for further exclusivity to consider. A further two months passed before the agent finally got back to us with a "thanks but no thanks" rejection. Four months wasted. Fortunately, we had stuck it on Amazon as an e-book.

During those four months the book the agents said would never sell notched up more than 60,000 sales on Kindle UK alone, reached number two (out of 950,000 titles) on three occasions, and acquired more than 100 five-star reviews.

Time was Saffina Desforges couldn't get the time of day from a major agent; Now some of the biggest agents going call us, and not from Britain—from New York. But agents move at a glacial pace and publishers even more so. The future is digital. That's not to say we would reject a legacy-publisher offer, but as successful e-authors we can negotiate from a position of strength and argue our case. We've proven a market exists for our works.

Don't fall for the myths about agents and publishers not touching self-published works. We've been head-hunted by one of the most prestigious agencies on the planet. Six months ago they wouldn't have given us the time of day. And we're not the exception. E-books are the new query. Prove your book has a readership and can make money and the legacy guys will not be far behind.

Amazon US: amzn.to/mOkjqa
Amazon UK: amzn.to/lhC5BR
Website: markwilliamsinternational.com

22. Shayne Parkinson

I've never tried the traditional publishing route. Years ago I asked someone in publishing if it would be worth my while submitting my books. He assured me there would be absolutely no interest in my long historical novels set in New Zealand. As the thought of the whole submission/long wait/probable rejection process didn't appeal anyway, I was happy enough to leave it at that. I let the books circulate through a network of friends and acquaintances; I wrote more; I stacked the print-outs on the bottom shelf of a bookcase and let them gather dust.

And then e-publishing arrived. Not only was it possible to put your own e-books online, it was easy. It didn't matter whether you lived in New York or New Zealand. It seemed worth a try. I dusted off the books and gave them a thorough going-over. I put the first one on a site with beta readers from several different countries, took note of trends in the responses, and made substantial editorial changes. After yet another polishing pass, the books were ready to be launched on Smashwords.

Nothing happened for months. Oh, there were a few sales, and an occasional review. But I was one unknown author among thousands, with nothing to make me stand out.

Things started to pick up when I made the first book free, and after a few months I started to see the results of word-of-mouth among readers. I've now had more than 30,000 downloads of that first book at Smashwords, and dozens of reviews. Their retail distribution has put the books in several other outlets, and I've been delighted at the response, especially on Barnes & Noble. Late in April 2011 my books appeared in the Kindle store. I had a stroke of luck in May, with Amazon price-matching to make the first book free, and soon after that the other three books made it into the Top 100 for historical fiction.

I'm not a natural marketer. I enjoy interacting with people, and I enjoy writing. I've benefited hugely from word-of-mouth. Two years ago I'd never have believed that I'd be regularly getting fan mail from around the world.

Every writer's experience is subtly different. For me, the most important things have been: making the books as good as I possibly can; being accessible—the books are in a variety of outlets, I've a website and a blog, and an easy-to-find e-mail address; patience; and, a healthy dose of luck.

Website: bit.ly/kKy4dU
Amazon: amzn.to/jwh8Xo

23. *Stacey Wallace Benefiel*

I've been a self-published author for a little over a year and I think I've had a pretty typical journey.

After querying the first novel in my YA paranormal romance trilogy on and off from 2005 to 2010 and getting upwards of 70 rejections, I was ready to give up. Agents and publishers said they liked *Glimpse*, but they always suggested what they would change. Each time I received a suggestion I changed the manuscript and then sent the pages or, in a couple of cases, the whole manuscript back to them. Still no-one signed me.

For Christmas 2009, my husband gave me a Kindle. I blew through my accompanying Amazon gift card in two days, purchasing several e-books from traditional publishers. When I'd finished reading them, I trolled Amazon for some cheaper reads and found plenty of e-books that interested me in the 99c to $5.00 price range. I particularly enjoyed *Kept* by Zoe Winters and I googled her to find out who her publisher was.

When I discovered that *Kept* was self-published I was elated. I set about learning everything I could about self-publishing and in April of 2010 I published *Glimpse*. I queried book bloggers for reviews; set up a Twitter account, a blog, a website, a Facebook page, and a Goodreads account; and I waited.

I sold 12 copies of *Glimpse* that first month and I couldn't believe this book I'd been trying to get published for five years was finally out there and people were buying it! I finished the second book in the trilogy, *Glimmer*, over the summer and readied it for publication in the fall. I also wrote a novelette for adults entitled *Day of Sacrifice,* just for kicks, and put it out two weeks before *Glimmer.* That's when my sales started gaining momentum.

By November 2010 I'd reached the important milestone of selling 1,000+ e-books a month. I have been able to keep that going, but have seen some slowing this past spring. Instead of becoming preoccupied with my sales, I've buckled down and written more. There are three novelettes in the *Day of Sacrifice* series out at the moment and the fourth will be published this summer. I'm a few weeks away from publishing the last book in my YA trilogy, *Glow.* In May, I published a book of humorous essays entitled *The Toilet Business* and was thrilled to do so. If I'd had an agent or a publisher, I'm sure they would have discouraged me from working on things outside of my usual genre.

I may not be the greatest success story in self-publishing, but I have a career that I love and I am able to support my family of four on what I earn from my writing. I'm in this for the long-haul.

Amazon: amzn.to/keBRiZ
Website: staceywallacebenefiel.com

24. Sarah Woodbury

Academic writing has been a way of life for me for a long time, but writing fiction was another story. I wrote my first novel in the spring of 2006 on a whim, just to see if I could. My daughter (then 14) had always been "the writer" in the family and I even asked her if it was okay if I gave it a shot too.

That first book was straight high fantasy (with elves, no less) and will never see the light of day. I knew at the time that it wasn't very good, but I didn't know how to fix the problems. Instead of trying, I launched into a second book, which eventually became *Footsteps in Time*—the first book in my time-travel fantasy series.

This one seemed to be much better written and more cohesive. When I thought I'd finished it, I started querying agents, completely unaware that a community of writers all doing the same thing existed online. One year and upwards of 72 rejections later, the very last agent I queried took me on. She did send my book to several publishers, but after eight months, and when I hadn't heard from her for most of the summer, I found out she'd closed her business without telling any of her clients.

In the interim, I had written the rest of the *After Cilmeri* series, *Prince of Time* and *Daughter of Time*. But now, without an agent and faced with the prospect of more query letters, I abandoned the series and wrote what became *The Last Pendragon* in the fall of 2008.

With this book I queried one agent, who loved the book and took me on (and still represents me). It seemed 2009 and 2010 were the worst years on record for trying to break in as an new author; he was unable to sell either *The Last Pendragon* or the sixth book I'd written, *Cold My Heart*.

In September of 2009, with my agent's blessing, I started giving *The Last Pendragon* away for free. At around 8,000 copies later, a fan sent me an e-mail urging me not to give away my book anymore and saying that she "would have gladly paid for it."

Thus, starting in January 2011, I became an indie author. Along with *The Last Pendragon*, I published a heavily edited and revised *Footsteps in Time* and *Prince of Time*, neither of which were doing me any good moldering on my laptop. I added *Daughter of Time* in March, and *Cold My Heart* in April.

After a typically slow beginning, with modest sales of fewer than 100 books in January and February, I sold closer to 500 books in March across all platforms, more than 3,000 in April, and over 4,000 in May. My indie publishing journey is off to a great start! Here's to many more years of writing and reading.

Webpage: sarahwoodbury.com
Amazon: tinyurl.com/3qde9ev
Barnes & Noble: tinyurl.com/3r33ahf
Apple: tinyurl.com/3wrjx8y

25. Kenneth Rosenberg

I wrote my first novel in 1990. I was very optimistic at the time. I figured I'd write it, get an agent, land a publishing deal, and be on my way. As it turned out, the first part of that equation was the only part I had any control over. I did manage to write it, but hundreds of query letters to agents and publishers over the next several years led nowhere. It was the beginning of a long, arduous road to rejection.

Over the next 20 years, I wrote five more novels and at least as many screenplays. I sent out hundreds of queries each time, but the result was always the same: absolutely no interest from anyone in the publishing industry. I'd considered the prospect of self-publishing over the years, but always figured that if I ever went that route it would mean I'd finally given up. Self-publishing was for people who wanted to pass copies out to friends and relatives. It was the end of all hope of actually earning a living from my writing.

That all changed, of course, with the advent of e-books. Starting around 2008 I began to keep an eye on this trend, although it wasn't until I saw some of the success stories of other independent authors in 2010 that I decided it was time to take the plunge. What did I have to lose? After 20 years of failure in the traditional publishing realm, I might as well give this new paradigm a shot.

The first thing that went through my mind was that this time my draft had to be absolutely the best effort I could possibly put forward. If I'd sold a book to a publishing company, it would be edited and revised and proofread. If I put it out on my own, it had to be as near perfect as I could make it. I set about revising my latest novel, *No Cure for the*

Broken Hearted. I spent about three months revising it for the umpteenth time, then passed it to friends who helped with editing, and then revised it again. Finally, in December 2010, it was ready to go.

Within two months, my book began racing up the bestseller lists, particularly in the UK, where it climbed as high as the number nine e-book on Amazon overall. Granted, my price was set at 99c (49p), but still, I was right up there in the Top Ten! Sharing space with Stieg Larsson, no less! And I was making actual money in the process.

Now I'm busy revising my next book, hoping to capitalize on whatever momentum I've managed to build. I know that success as an independent author takes equal parts skill, determination, hard work, and luck. And with enough of the first three, I think you can make your own luck!

Amazon: amzn.to/ju9meT
Website: kennethrosenberg.com

26. Katie Klein

I originally decided to e-pub because I felt I was out of options. The market was extremely volatile, I was on an agent hunt, and no one seemed to be responsive. By the time I decided to upload *Cross My Heart* (a young adult contemporary romance), I'd accrued 75 agent rejections (some never responded, some rejected the query, some the partial, and three rejected it after reading the final version). It was never the writing, or the story. It was always the "market." More specifically, they weren't sure it would "stand out" enough. I loved Parker and Jaden, though, and I believed in their story. I felt if I loved these two people (who aren't even real!) this much, then someone out there was bound to feel the same way.

I stayed on the sidelines for a few months before I jumped on the e-pub "train." I lurked around the Kindle Boards and followed J. A. Konrath's blog posts. I was really interested in how others were faring (what was working and what wasn't). I didn't rush into anything and kept very realistic expectations. I didn't believe the stories where "no name" authors found an audience for their novels, but I slapped a "no name" on the cover anyway, sat back, and waited.

Cross My Heart took off faster than I ever could have predicted. In the first three months, I sold more than 4,000 copies and hit the Amazon Teen Top 100. The response has been overwhelming. I worked hard to make *Cross My Heart* the best story it could possibly be, and publishing it on my own helped me reach thousands of new readers. The alternative was to let it sit languishing on my hard drive, read by no one. Every new piece of fan mail I get, and every four-and five-star review confirms I made the right decision.

It's impossible to predict the level of success any given indie writer will have, but, at the same time, there's nothing to lose in trying.

Amazon: amzn.to/kSoicJ
Website: katiekleinbooks.com
Blog: katiekleinwrites.blogspot.com

27. Nell Gavin

When I was writing *Threads: The Reincarnation of Anne Boleyn* in 2000, my choices were to go the traditional route with a mainstream publisher or try my luck with the new Print-on-Demand technology. E-books were out there, but they had a very limited audience that wasn't growing yet.

I opted for POD publishing, so I could retain control, and I selected a POD publisher that offered a lower retail price than some of the others, and a contract that gave me 100% of the rights to the book. Sales were relatively low for years but were always steady. I knew my book appealed to a niche market, not a mass market, so I let it find its audience in its own time and at its own speed. I knew a traditional publisher would never have had the patience to do that and would have made me change the story to appeal to more people or yanked the title after a few months. I'd worked too hard for that.

The thing is, self-publishing is forever, so even low sales never meant having my book taken out of print. I met a number of traditionally published authors who accepted— and didn't even question—that the life cycle of their books was only five months to one year. They shrugged and kept writing, knowing their work had a very short lifespan and made them very little money. What they *did* have, I noticed, was bragging rights because they had been published. Was that worth relinquishing control and accepting a premature death for my book?

I felt one year wasn't nearly long enough to find my audience. I also knew that I was actually selling more books each month than many of the traditionally published authors

I met. I listened to them complain about their publishers, their agents, and the treatment their books received in bookstores and was grateful I had less aggravation than they did. Losing my bragging rights was a small price to pay.

Later, I joined the first wave of Kindle authors and sold perhaps five to nine books a month for a year. Then that number crept up at Christmas to about one copy per day and then crept up again the following Christmas. When Amazon lowered the price of the Kindle, sales exploded, and they kept rising.

I changed my cover art when my son, who had created the original art, was old enough to not have his feelings hurt. Overnight—with nothing but a new cover—the book began to sell more and more and more, and my sales figures kept rising. It kept creeping up the category lists until *Threads* was in the Top 10 for every category that displayed on its Amazon book page. On the UK site, it's typically #1. All this happened after the book had been available for 10 years.

Over the years, I signed with two agents (one in the US and one in Europe), had three unsolicited movie option offers, and had a version sold and translated into Italian. All this occurred when I was still selling a comparatively small number of POD books and wasn't bothering with any kind of promotion. It taught me that even a very obscure book by an unknown author can find its way to movie producers and agents.

During those years I learned a lot about self-publishing. It is not a dead end, and it is not a failure; it's the best option for control freaks (like me) who write things that not everyone will understand or know how to market.

Most importantly, I learned that you cannot do it alone—you need a community of other authors to answer your questions, give you advice, and sympathize with you when you get that first bad review. Regardless of what you earn or how many books you sell, or what kinds of reviews you receive, the process is a very rich learning experience on a number of levels. It is also a very fun one!

Amazon: amzn.to/jdi4NF

28. Martin C. Sharlow

I started my self-publishing career at the end of December 2009. I had been working on a story for a few years by that time. I'd write for a bit and then put it away for great lengths of time. I always heard that getting published was as hard as hitting it big in acting, so I never intended on trying to get published. It wasn't even a concept for me until I started finding writing groups on the internet. I thought it was cool that all these people hung out and socialized about something none of them would ever really do.

That was until a few of them actually got published. It blew me away. How could these people have been so lucky? This led to me doing some research on the subject and to me finding other groups that had more information about getting published. In time, I found myself on Authonomy and learning about queries and agents. The more I learned about it, the more it seemed like a waste of time. I began to see that maybe I had been right to begin with. I've never been much of a follower. I almost always take the other road when it comes to doing things. It's caused me no small pain in my life, but it has been a great source of pride as well.

During this period of research, I came across Amazon's Kindle Publishing. At first I thought it was a scam. After all, that's what seems to be so prevalent these days, and it seemed just too good to be true. I put it aside for a few months before deciding to do more research. When I did, I was surprised to find an entire group of authors at Kindle Boards. There I learned all about how Kindle Publishing wasn't a scam, but really quite legitimate. At this time I was already beginning to send out queries to agents and receiving the common responses (and non-responses) all writers experience.

I wasn't sure when it went from just writing for fun to deciding I wanted to be published. I'm sure the Authonomy crowd had something to do with that. Whatever the reason, I knew I wanted to be published, and the fact that the agent route could take years just didn't sit well with me. I've always been a trailblazer so why change now? I have to admit I was nervous when I went for Kindle Publishing.

Everyone screamed I would ruin my writing future by sticking myself with the "self-published" label. In the end, I went for it. I'm glad I did. Since publishing on the Kindle, I've sold around 15,000 books. I am currently making a living writing books, and I am sure if I went the traditional way I'd still be sitting where I was, waiting for my career to finally start.

I'm glad I took the plunge.

Amazon: amzn.to/kD85iQ

29. William Esmont

"Don't waste your time. Real publishers won't touch you if they discover you've self-published." This is the advice I received from a friend when I first floated the idea of going independent in mid-2008. The Kindle had just launched and the blogosphere was abuzz with the potential of e-books. Despite the hype, it was clear that no-one, except maybe Jeff Bezos, had any idea of the truly disruptive potential of this new gadget.

I had been writing novels for about four years by this point, and I had two completed stories languishing on my hard drive, along with a respectable pile of rejection letters from various literary agencies. I was itching to try something different, to take matters into my own hands.

Unfortunately, I listened to that advice. I buckled down and continued writing query letters. And waiting. And waiting... It took me another year of near-misses before I finally mustered the courage to go digital.

The first two months on Kindle were brutal. I sold a total of three books. That's right— three. I had no idea what I was doing. My cover art was atrocious. Editing and proofreading were non-existent. I ended up pulling my novel from Amazon at the end of February 2010 and slinking back to my office, fully prepared to continue the query-and-wait process. I wanted nothing to do with marketing and publicity. I was a writer after all, not a businessman.

But then something magical happened. In May of 2010, I stumbled across a web forum called Kindle Boards. Much to my astonishment, Kindle Boards was full of authors like myself, people who had a story to tell and a new medium in which to do it. These were people who were comfortable with the technology, yet novices at the arcane world of publishing. I quickly became obsessed with the Writer's Cafe, logging in daily to follow the adventures of these other pioneers.

Meanwhile, I was busy working on my next book, an espionage thriller titled *The Patriot Paradox*. This time around, I entered the process with my eyes wide open. I made a business plan. I arranged for blog reviews and conducted giveaways on popular sites such as Goodreads. I became both an author and a businessman.

The Patriot Paradox went live in late October of 2010. In November I sold 37. December saw 84. In February, thanks to a Kindle Nation Daily sponsorship, I sold 768. Then things got really interesting. March came in at 3,233 and almost doubled again in April, reaching 6,434 copies.

What's next? Write more books. I'm hard at work on the sequel to *The Patriot Paradox* and I just launched the first in my zombie horror series. With luck, sales will continue. But even if they don't, I'll still be writing. It's who I am.

Amazon: amzn.to/kjR2zX
Website: williamesmont.com
Twitter: twitter.com/WilliamEsmont

30. Lexi Revellian

For a new writer, having a self-published book on Amazon is like being a pretty girl at a party where most of the other women are celebrities—and one or two in the corner are taking their tops off. It's remarkable, then, that any of us manage to sell our books at all—but we do. Even the indie's main weapon, a low price, is up against freebies and special offers from the Big Six publishers.

I never meant to self-publish. I wrote three books, each better than the last, and I knew the third, *Remix*, was publishable. It's a contemporary mystery/romance, a feel-good page-turner. Unfortunately, in spite of interest from agents, two of whom approached me, at the end of the year none had taken me on. With a heavy heart and gritted teeth I published on Amazon in August 2010. I was lucky. After a hesitant start, the book took off, and in my best month that single title sold 5,940 e-copies.

As sales slowed, I finished my next novel, *Replica*, a thriller/romance. In its first seven weeks it sold 5,000 copies. At the time of writing, more than 34,000 people have bought a book written by me, a fact I find incredibly satisfying.

What does the future hold? Publishing is in a state of turmoil, with bookshop chains failing, agents turning to publishing, mainstream authors going indie and vice versa. Sometimes I fear that this may be a brief golden era for self-publishers, before the Big Six work out how to squash us like bugs. At other times I think we are unstoppable.

Amazon UK: amzn.to/iZrzhm
Amazon US: amzn.to/loiyN2
Website: lexirevellian.com
Blog: lexirevellian.blogspot.com

31. J Carson Black

If I had a badge it would say: I Am a Proud Team Member

They say writing is a solitary business, and that's true when it comes to writing the book itself. But I've had a lot of help getting to the milestone I reached today. At the time of writing (June 5, 2011), I've sold a little more than 100,000 Kindle e-books—and that's just for the year so far. There are many reasons for this, but the pivotal moment for me came last summer when my husband Glenn decided to (a) get my rights back from my former publishers, and (b) put those books up on Amazon Kindle.

Without that step (which I initially thought of as a waste of time—I made one sale in June and 2 sales in July) we'd still be looking under the couch seats for change. I owe a huge debt of gratitude to Glenn, because without him none of this would have happened.

My journey has probably been easier than most and that's because my husband and best friend worked tirelessly to get the books up. Turns out we're a pretty good team. We see eye-to-eye on the covers, and both of us have art backgrounds. We discuss our goals and can change them if we have to. Because we didn't have much money, we did everything ourselves. We purchased photos, studied the latest hardcover thrillers from the Big Six publishers, tweaked the product descriptions as we went along, and decided the specific character of each book and the best way to market it. Who's the audience for this book? Can they tell from the cover what kind of book this will be? We presented a unified front, and the books, I believe, reflect that view.

I read somewhere that the best solution is out there somewhere, but most companies don't have the time nor the resources to find that sweet spot. There might be 100 different things they can try, one of which turns out to be best for the company's success and bottom line. Glenn and I consider ourselves fortunate that we are small and agile. We can try a price change and give it a little time to see the result. We try a lot of things—some work, some don't. But being nimble is one of the best aspects of e-book publishing. I think that's why there are so many success stories—you have only to go to Kindle Boards' Writers Café to see them. When it's your book, your name, and you are responsible for marketing it, you will do your level best because you have real skin in the game. You become your own best advocate and your own best client.

For us, our team effort is working out great. After 30 years of marriage, who knew?

Website: jcarsonblack.com
Amazon: amzn.to/nEDcmq

32. Imogen Rose

Eighteen months ago I didn't even know what a Kindle was. I wasn't looking to publish my story *Portal* (a YA time travel story), which I had written for my daughter. I was really only looking for a way to get it bound (those Staples bindings were too bulky!) and I accidentally found Createspace.

I got *Portal* formatted and ready to print as a paperback. Imagine my delight when I discovered that I could hit a "publish" button and have it displayed on Amazon! I visited the Createspace forum and from there checked out boards like Kindle Boards and Mobileread. I then went on to publish my books on Kindle and later on Nook.

Portal morphed into a series (the *Portal Chronicles*), and there are now four books in the series with one yet to be written. I also started on a second series, the *Bonfire Chronicles* (YA paranormal) with *Faustine* being the first book in that series.

It was a slow start, but sales quickly picked up and before I knew it I was selling thousands a month. I began to get e-mails from film producers and literary agents wanting to know if I had representation. I instantly connected with Mollie Glick from Foundry Media, who contacted me via my website.

We have since hooked up with Michelle Weiner (CAA) who is looking into the film/tv opportunities that have come my way. Mollie and I are looking to shop my first series this coming fall. It's really exciting times!

Website: imogenrose.com
Twitter: twitter.com/ImogenRoseTweet

Website: imogenrose.com
Twitter: twitter.com/ImogenRoseTweet
Blog: imogenroseblog.blogspot.com
Amazon: amzn.to/k9kMAf

33. Mark Edwards

As I write this, a novel I co-wrote with Louise Voss, *Catch Your Death*, is sitting at #2 on the Amazon Kindle bestseller list. Our other thriller, *Killing Cupid*, is #7. As far as I know, we are the first 100% indie novelists to ever have two novels in the Amazon UK Top 10, and have equaled the highest position achieved by the other successful indie crime-writing duo, Saffina Desforges, with their thriller *Sugar and Spice*. Only David Belbin stands between us and the #1 slot.

Worldwide, there have been a number of high-profile indie writers who have struck gold since Amazon introduced their self-publishing platform: Amanda Hocking, John Locke, and HP Mallory to name a few. And Stephen Leather has sold an eye-watering number of downloads, but he is an established writer with a large fan base. So how did we do it?

A few years ago, Louise and I wrote *Killing Cupid*—a stalker novel with a twist. A lucky break led to us getting the novel optioned by the BBC, but it never got made. We then wrote our second novel, *Catch Your Death*, a Dan Brown-style conspiracy thriller. We were proud of them, but *Catch Your Death* was completed the same week as my first daughter was born. Real life got in the way and we never made much of an effort to find an agent or publisher.

Then, last autumn, I was bought a Kindle for my birthday and, having read about a few authors who had found a large audience through self-publishing, I persuaded Louise that we should give it a go. What did we have to lose? We spent a few months re-writing the novels, updating them to include new-fangled technology like Facebook and smartphones, and put *Killing Cupid* live this February. On day one we sold a single copy—to my girlfriend's mum. Fortunately, she liked it.

We then embarked on a mission to sell as many copies as possible. We blogged, we networked, we did interviews, wrote articles, joined forums and annoyed the hell out of our friends on Facebook and Twitter. In March we sold 113 copies. We were overjoyed. Sales ticked along throughout April at about 10–20 a day, until the final few days of the month when we picked up momentum and increased sales to 50 a day. We became addicted to checking our sales figures. We leapt up to #171 in the charts. Ecstasy!

Slowly, slowly, like a tortoise making its own sweet way to the finishing line, *Killing Cupid* plodded up the charts. It finally broke into the Top 100 in mid-May. We set our targets high: 1,000 copies a month. That would do us. We picked up some great reviews from readers. "I never knew there were such good books on Kindle," said one, making our year.

Three weeks ago, we put our second novel, *Catch Your Death* (for fans of Dan Brown and Stieg Larsson), live. This, we always believed, was the more commercial of the two, with a fast-paced plot revolving around a killer virus and a Harvard virologist. It shot into the chart at #5,000.

Then something incredible happened. A week ago, *Killing Cupid* entered the Top 50 and starting climbing into the 20s. Dreams were coming true. Plod, plod, up the chart. And then this Saturday *Catch Your Death* went whoosh. Rather like a hare, in fact. It shot up from #120 to #9 in less than 48 hours. The tortoise crawled along behind it. This afternoon, we overtook Karin Slaughter to land at #2. I almost passed out with excitement. Yesterday alone, we sold more than 1,500 books.

I came up with the idea of adding the subtitle (for fans of Dan Brown and Stieg Larsson) because I wanted something that would catch the eye of thriller readers when they were browsing Amazon, and the novel has a similar theme of solving a mystery through delving into the past and a fast pace. I have no idea if it's affected sales. I think that most sales have come from readers of *Killing Cupid*, which has been selling steadily for months. Those readers all bought *Catch Your Death* in a burst, sending it up the charts, and we have a very strong blurb, an eye-catching cover and a clever title.

What happens next? I have no idea. Right now, we are enjoying being (almost) on top of the world (well, the UK). The Kindle is now officially my favorite gadget ever and for many indie authors like us, it's been a godsend. As they say on The X Factor, "we've been on an amazing journey," and all without a single sighting of Simon Cowell's chest.

Postscript: An hour after I wrote the above, *Catch Your Death* hit the #1 spot. A week later, it was still there. It's been unbelievably exciting. The first true indies to hit #1. And to stay there for a week is extraordinary, even if I'm convinced it's all going to end any minute. But we have now sold more than 21,000 e-books—18,000 of them in two weeks! On one extraordinary day in June 2011, *Catch Your Death* sold 1900 copies! I couldn't believe what I was seeing.

The message I want to impart is that if you are good enough, smart enough, and determined enough, you can do it. And you can do it without being nasty and without trying to put anyone else down. One of the best things about this whole experience so far has been how many good friends I've made in the indie world. People like Mark Williams (half of Saffina Desforges), HP Mallory, Dan Holloway, Allan Guthrie, J Carson Black, Victorine Lieske, Sibel Hodge, Steven Saville... the list goes on and on. All great, thoroughly nice people, joined together by a love of writing and a shared dream.

Although if any of them dare knock us off that number one spot... ;)

Website: indieiq.com

Appendix A—Shorter Stories

The short story has been "dying" for at least as long as the publishing industry has. Most articles can't even mention it without pronouncing it as "moribund" or defending its "rude health." People either devour short stories, or ignore them. But what is it about the humble short that divides opinion so?

Short stories have had a huge impact on popular culture. Some of the greatest writers, such as Edgar Allen Poe, practiced the form exclusively. Others, including Anton Chekhov, Luis Borges, Stephen King, Franz Kafka, William Trevor, and Kurt Vonnegut count their shorter pieces as some of their finest work.

Many famous movies have been adapted from short stories. *Memento* was originally a fine short story written by the director's brother, Jonathan Nolan. Others include *The Body Snatcher*, *Stand By Me*, *2001: A Space Odyssey*, *Brokeback Mountain*, *Total Recall*, *The Curious Case of Benjamin Button*, *The Fly*, *Zorro*, *Minority Report*, *Million Dollar Baby*, *The Illusionist*, and *I, Robot*. Quite an eclectic list.

Maybe that list tells us something about the short story. The form, generally defined as anything below 10,000 words (but usually a lot less), allows writers to experiment, write outside their genres, and try something new. A writer is free to gamble with a short story, because if the story ends up not working, its author has wasted only a few days rather than a few months.

So why all the naysayers? One of the traditional paths to success for an aspiring novelist was to have a short story published in one of the top magazines (e.g. *The Atlantic*, *The*

New Yorker) or one of the top literary journals (e.g. *Glimmer Train, Tin House*). This publishing credit would be enough to attract the attention of a top agent, and the healthy paycheck would be more than enough to survive on while the author wrote more. While this is still a valid way to break into the industry, the readership for short fiction in magazines seems to have fallen away. Many magazine editors complain they have more writers submitting than people reading, and pay rates have fallen as a result.

Today, professional rates for short stories are considered to be $0.05 a word or higher (but not that much higher). For a 2,000-word short story, that's $100. Even if you were prolific enough to churn out a few stories a week, edit them, submit them to professional markets, and have them all accepted, you couldn't live off the money. While there are higher-paying markets, the competition is fierce and even popular writers with long publishing histories get rejected all the time.

Short story collections don't sell nearly as well as novels, and agents and publishers aren't going to be interested in them unless you already have a name, or your stories have been published in the very top publications (and even then it's a struggle).

This hasn't stopped some authors believing there is an untapped market out there for short stories. The reasoning behind this is seductive: people have shorter attention spans these days, and readers consume the written word in radically different ways. With smartphones, tablets, and netbooks, people may be once more gravitating towards shorter pieces.

With all the distractions from other, flashier forms of entertainment (sports, television, the internet), it can be a struggle to put aside an hour or two, find somewhere quiet, and read a book; whereas, short stories can be read in 20 minutes—while on the bus, enjoying a lunch break, or in the queue at the DMV. They can be read on a phone easily, without hurting the eyes, and the reader does not have to invest as much in the story. There is also less risk. Even if readers don't like it, at least they have invested little time or money in it.

Short stories are fun to write too. My first novel was historical fiction, as is the one I am working on at the moment, and the next two planned after that. Short stories allow me to write something different. They are a release. I don't have to spend two hours researching how long it takes to reload a musket; I just write, and it's liberating.

There are constraints to the form, however. There is only a limited amount of space, and even less time to hook the reader, but this can make for powerful work. One of Hemingway's most famous stories was just six words long—"For Sale: Baby Shoes, Never Worn."

Short Story Markets

Whether you write short stories or novels, or anything in between, there are a number of different markets available. If you are aiming to make a living from your stories, or at least supplement your income, you should be aware of all of them.

You can sell a short story to magazines, both online and offline, and receive a fee in return. Rates start at nothing or a few free copies of the publication, right up to professional rates of $0.05 a word or more. Typically, stories between 2,000 words and 4,000 words are the most marketable, but there's demand for all lengths.

Duotrope.com is an excellent search engine for short story markets and I use it often. Results can be filtered by genre, pay-rates, and so on. It's also great if you have something of an awkward length, such a novella, as you can search for places that accept longer works of fiction. Ralan.com is another site, although it is geared more towards science-fiction, horror, and fantasy. If you write in those genres, you should check it out.

Writers' forums are excellent resources for short story

writers and provide plenty of information on what editors are looking for and how they prefer submissions to be made. Forums are also support networks filled with writers of all levels, and you can find some experienced beta readers there too. Refer to the *Resources* section at the end of the book for some suggestions.

Generally, magazines pay for "first rights," meaning the story cannot have been published anywhere else, even on your own website. How and when rights will revert to you is usually spelled out in the contract. Sometimes, if your story is to be published in print, such "first rights" may be limited to print versions in a particular country or territory. Works posted on critique forums are mostly considered unpublished and exempt, as long as anything posted to forums remains hidden from search engine bots in a password-protected section. For more information on copyright, please see the *Practicalities* section.

Publishing in magazines can be great for enhancing your writer's CV and for seeing your name in print for the first time, but don't expect to make a living out of it. If you are planning on querying an agent, a credit from a well-known magazine will help—at the very least, the agent may read your query thinking it might be interesting rather than assuming it's probably going to be awful.

The main drawback to magazines is that they often run on a very tight budget. As a result, staff struggle to cope with the amount of submissions, so hearing back can take anything from a week to a year, although two to three months is standard. Some markets allow simultaneous submissions; some require exclusives. Make sure you check first.

It's crucial to follow submission guidelines exactly, and read a copy of the magazine first. Submitting without knowing what kind of stories the editor likes is probably wasting the editor's time as well as your own, especially if it's a competitive market.

I sold the first short story I wrote—*The Boy With the Extra Toe* (which was later renamed)—to a small UK literary magazine called *The Delinquent*. They didn't pay anything, but it was a great boost seeing my name in print, and gave me confidence at a difficult time in my writing career.

After you have sold the first rights to a story, there are a small number of magazines you can sell the same story to again, although it is usually good form to wait a little after the first publication, so as not to cannibalize the first magazine's sales. Rates are usually, but not always, less than what you receive for first rights, but it's great to get paid again for the same story when all you have to do is to submit it. It's another publication credit on your CV, and it brings you more readers, which is what this is all about. Duotrope will allow you to search for markets that accept reprints.

I sold the reprint rights to my first story to an online short story website called Short Story America. The site pays a flat rate (whether stories are reprints or not) of $100, and reserves the right to display the story for as long as they like on the website. The rights granted were non-exclusive, meaning I could self-publish the story or even sell the reprint again (although few editors would be interested in a story that is free online). While having the story freely available online may limit potential reprint sales in future, I was happy to trade the small chance of selling the story again for the increased exposure. If you are in a similar position, ensure you check the contract to determine what rights you are granting and whether it will impede further use or sale of your story in any way, and factor that into your decision to sell.

Editors regularly put together collections (often on a single theme) and put out a call for submissions. Again, pay rates range from nothing, to free copies, to a flat rate, or royalties from sales. If you sign up to Duotrope's newsletter, you will get a monthly list of available markets. Sometimes editors will want first rights, sometimes they don't mind if a story has been once published before or even several times. Check before submitting. One of my stories, *If You Go into the Woods*, came out in a fancy hardback collection in June, also published by Short Story America. They are planning paperback, e-book, and audio versions (both CD and MP3), and I will receive royalties on those sales once costs are covered. The point is, there is more than one way to sell the same story, and you can often sell it more than once.

Selling short story collections to publishing houses is very, very difficult. If you aren't already traditionally published (with commendable sales figures), you will likely struggle to interest an agent in a collection. Linked collections may have a greater chance of success, but not by much.

Publishing a collection of short stories probably isn't a realistic option for most novice writers, especially if they haven't gained an MFA from a prestigious university, or are at an early stage in their careers. If you think that's unfair, ask yourself this: when was the last time you bought a short story collection by an unknown writer?

Maximizing Your Short Story Income

As mentioned, there are many ways to sell the same story if you are smart and do it in the correct order, so if you write short stories exclusively, or have a lot of them on your hard drive, you might consider setting up a system where you sell first rights, then reprint/anthology rights, and only then consider self-publishing. Remember, once you publish them online, your first rights are gone, and you may severely restrict reprint or anthology options. I've decided to depart from that strategy a little for now, but I plan to return that system (or a version of it) in the future. If you do choose to self-publish, don't forget that mentioning in the blurb that the short story has already been published in a magazine can add serious weight to the description.

Novellas

If I were to tell you a story about the first time I went to Brazil, I would tell you about the time I woke up face-to-face with the severed head of a bull. I wouldn't tell you about the weeks beforehand, when I did nothing but laze on the beach drinking too much, or the months of trying to decide what flight to buy and wondering whether I needed malaria pills. My point is that I'd start the story *exactly* when it gets interesting, and end it *before* it started to get boring.

But how long should that story be? That depends on the story, but traditionally the writer's options have been limited. Market forces and cost considerations have tended to straitjacket a writer so that the only acceptable length was a short story or a novel. A short story is generally defined as anything shorter than 10,000 words. Some people say 7,500 words, others say 20,000, but I think 10,000 is pretty standard as an upper limit.

For novels, the length preferred by publishers and agents is 80,000 to 100,000 words, with slight variations for genre. (Children's chapbooks and Young Adult novels are generally slightly shorter at upwards of 35,000 words.) There are good reasons for adhering to prescribed lengths. First of all, the longer the book, the more it costs to print. The higher the printing costs, the higher the book's price. Naturally, most readers will balk at a very high-priced book, even a long one, especially if you aren't JK Rowling or Stephen King. Conversely, readers risking their cash on an unknown writer will want to know they are getting at least a few hours of entertainment and will look askance at a thin read.

Successful writers can break these rules (let's face it, *really* successful writers can pretty much do whatever they want), but the other 99% have to play the game. Most agents won't even look at a book outside these word-count guidelines if it is written by an unpublished author. If your word count is 150,000 or more, an agent probably won't even read your query letter, let alone your manuscript. If you're lucky, you'll get a curt message advising you to trim your book, but that's it.

Over the years, however, many classic works have been produced outside of these restrictions. On the longer side you have *War & Peace* (460,000), *Les Misérables* (510,000), *Middlemarch* (315,000), and two I thought were shorter, *Catch-22* (175,000) and *Crime & Punishment* (210,000). These books are either doorstoppers or published in tiny fonts (or both) and were all first published before the corporatization of the publishing world.

If you are a new novelist or your sales are modest, a publisher will rarely risk producing a more expensive book when there are thousands of other eager authors with perfect-sized novels. Detailed cost assessments are made on every book before an editor makes an offer, so most will be wary of work that falls outside the average length. For this reason, one form has fallen by the wayside completely in the modern publishing world—the novella. Generally between 10,000 and 40,000 words (unless you allow a separate classification for "novelettes" which are between short stories and novellas), this form has produced a string of well-known classics: *A Christmas Carol*, *Of Mice and Men*, *Billy Budd*, *Animal Farm*, *Breakfast at Tiffany's*, *A Clockwork Orange*, *The Old Man and the Sea*, and *Heart of Darkness*.

Unfortunately, it is not economical for publishing houses to produce novellas because, although they have fewer pages, which means editorial and print costs are reduced, the publisher still has fixed costs such as cover design and marketing regardless of length. Customers expect to pay less for something half the size, meaning publishers' margins shrink to the point where it's only worthwhile publishing a novella if it will be a runaway hit.

So what is a writer to do? Up until recently, that meant either stretching or cutting your story to make it fit the preferred length. But, as mentioned earlier, a story should be whatever length makes it the most gripping. You know, the *right* length. I'm sure there are novels on everyone's bookshelves that would have been better if the writer hadn't padded it out, or omitted killer scenes to fit a certain length. I'm equally sure there are thousands more great stories we never even got to read because of these restrictions.

Well, not anymore.

With digital publishing, length doesn't matter as much. As there are no print costs, you can tell your story in the length it takes to tell the story. You don't have to add unnecessary subplots to pad it out, and you don't have to cut that scene you were so fond of to trim it down. You can tell the story your way—the way it was meant to be told.

While we haven't seen a boom in *War & Peace*-length novels (maybe they are still being written!), digital publishing has rekindled interest in the novella, and if this leads to the publication of new classics, such as those named above, everyone wins.

Appendix B—The International Market

Most of the companies and events driving change, to date, have been American. While the US is far ahead of the world in terms of e-reader and e-book adoption rates, it is where the rest of the world is headed (at greater or lesser speeds).

Amazon Surcharge

Writers often wonder why the growth of e-books is so much slower outside of the US. There are a several reasons, but I believe one big factor is the $2 surcharge Amazon levies on e-books in most international countries. This charge has nothing to do with taxes. It is levied by Amazon and kept by Amazon, and it applies whether the user downloads e-books through a Kindle or not (and whether the user even *owns* a Kindle or not). There is very little awareness of this issue, which is why I think it should be highlighted.

I was first made aware of the "Amazon Surcharge" by a reader from Hungary, who wanted to know why my 4,000-word, 99c e-book was costing him $3.44. He also wanted to know whether I received any of the extra money he was being charged. I wasn't, of course. In fact, I didn't know what he was talking about. However, after a little investigation, I discovered Amazon was applying a $2 surcharge on all e-books in most international countries.

If you live in the USA, Canada, the UK, Ireland, Australia, New Zealand, or the "Amazon Germany" countries (Germany, Austria, Switzerland, Luxembourg, and Liechtenstein), you escape this surcharge. However, if you live *anywhere else*, you will be forced to pay extra. In fact, the surcharge used to be applied much more widely and was only removed from the Amazon Germany countries when the Kindle was officially launched there in April 2010. It used to apply in Ireland, Australia, New Zealand, and Canada, but was also dropped sometime in 2010.

If you read e-books and live in one of these countries, this drastically affects how much you pay. If you are a writer and are selling internationally (and you should be, this is a global US$80 billion business), this is harming your sales right now. If you don't think this is a big deal because your books aren't translated into other languages anyway, you are missing the point. Millions of readers worldwide enjoy reading books published in English. In some countries, such as Denmark, the original English versions outsell translated versions. Also, many emerging economies, such as Brazil, lack a bookstore infrastructure, which means that publishers have to resort to methods such as selling door-to-door. These countries should be ripe for e-books, but Amazon is suffocating their growth.

When you go to Amazon.com and search for my short story e-books, you will see a price of $0.99, $1.16 or $3.44, depending on where you live. Whatever you pay, I get just $0.35 and, aside from around 15% in sales taxes, Amazon keeps the rest.

Let me be clear. This is *nothing* to do with sales tax or VAT. Sales tax (VAT) is levied on top of this surcharge. My short story e-books cost $0.99 in the US because no sales tax is currently levied by Amazon. The same e-books cost $1.16 in Ireland (which is not one of the surcharge countries) because Amazon is obliged to add 15% VAT (sales tax), and they seem to add a couple of cents more for "delivery costs".

However, for readers in surcharge-affected countries (which means most of the world), my e-books cost $3.44. This breaks down as: $0.99 + Amazon Surcharge of $2 = $2.99. 15% VAT (sales tax) is then added on top of that, giving a total price charged to the reader of $3.44.

To verify what I am saying, all you need do is log out of your Amazon account, fake your IP to, say, a Swedish address, then look at the prices in the Kindle Store. Some books seem to escape the surcharge—Amazon's system seems to miss them somehow—but it catches almost all new books.

So Why a Surcharge?

Now we have established this surcharge has nothing to do with taxes, and none of it is going to the author, what is it for? There is no point asking Amazon. I have e-mailed them several times about this, but they have never responded.

Some of my readers have done the same and been fobbed off with bogus excuses about higher operating costs in certain countries. Clearly this is patently untrue. There is no cost difference for Amazon between selling my e-book to a customer in France or to one in Kentucky, especially when that customer is using the Amazon.com site and downloading the book with their own computer on their own internet connection.

At first, I thought this surcharge only affected Kindle owners—that it was a surcharge for downloading books wirelessly because they bought their Kindle in the UK or the US and are using it in another country. Amazon *might* have had *some* justification for that. However, this is not the case. It affects all purchasers of e-books in those countries, whether they own a Kindle or not.

This issue affects all writers (and publishers), but affects self-published writers disproportionately. One of the key advantages "indie" writers have is the ability to be flexible on price. A self-publisher can price books at $0.99 or $2.99 and survive. Trade publishers can reduce the price of select titles for a limited time, but they can't do it with their entire list because they simply have too many overheads. Adding $2 to the price of a $12.99 e-book will have some impact on sales, for sure, but adding it to a $0.99 or $2.99 book, and then adding 15% VAT, just *kills* them.

Since I discovered this issue, I have been directing overseas readers to purchase my books on Smashwords or iTunes, where there is no surcharge. Smashwords has consequently gone from being an insignificant portion of my sales to almost 10% (and even more in revenue because they pay me $0.56 per copy sold instead of $0.35). And that's just the readers I am reaching with this message. How many international readers are balking because they think my books are overpriced? Of course, there is a much larger issue here than my immediate bottom line. This charge is slowing the growth of e-books all across the world.

Why this Charge Is So Dumb

One of the biggest drivers of e-reader adoption is lower priced e-books; however, cheap e-books largely don't exist in surcharge-affected countries. Because independent and small e-publishers do not exert the same downward price pressure, local publishers in the affected countries charge even more for e-books than they do in the US and the UK. Amazon's surcharge plays right into their hands.

In these countries, publishers are able to shore up print sales by discouraging e-reader adoption due to high e-book prices. What's particularly dumb about this is that it runs counter to Amazon's marketing strategy. In already developed e-book markets, Amazon is straining at the leash to drive prices down to encourage growth because most of Amazon's money is made in sales of the Kindle e-reader, not of e-books themselves. If Amazon dropped the surcharge, e-book sales would rise across the board. More people would purchase e-readers (including the Kindle), and the market could expand dramatically. In other words, Amazon's surcharge is hurting Amazon even more than it hurts authors. That's why it's so dumb.

The European Market

It's time to take a little trip around Europe. Before we look at some countries in more detail, let's look at some common aspects that are slowing growth across Europe (aside from the Amazon surcharge, which doesn't affect the two biggest book markets, the UK and Germany).

1. VAT (Sales Tax). The EU has two VAT rates. The low rate includes daily necessities (milk, newspapers) and other basics (print books, children's shoes). The higher rate covers luxury items (televisions, legal fees). While the EU allows member states to apply a low- or no-tax rate on the sale of printed books, e-books are erroneously classified as a "service" and are thus charged at the higher rate. Even though the EU issued a ruling in 2009 allowing member states to reduce the tax rate on e-books, few member states have followed suit. It should be noted that Amazon trade out of Luxembourg for tax purposes, hence the VAT rate applied by them to all EU purchases is 15%.

2. The e-reader market is competitive, but young. Apple is leading Amazon in some sectors, and Sony made early moves in others, but overall adoption rates are too low to give any guide as to which e-reader might come out on top in the future.

3. E-book sales in Europe, while increasing, have not seen anything like the explosion in the US. There are a number of reasons for this, including: the relatively high price of e-readers; high VAT on e-readers; high VAT on e-books; Amazon has a smaller share of the overall book market because of higher freight costs, taxes, and poorer overall broadband/wifi infrastructure; cultural differences, publisher resistance, and political interference. Despite these disadvantages, the market is still growing quickly.

4. The Kindle is only officially available in the UK and the Amazon Germany countries. Customers elsewhere can order it from the US, but it comes shipped with a US plug,

English-only menus and instructions (even in Germany), and significant delivery costs and customs charges.

5. Small publishing companies, and some self-publishers, are often barred from some distribution channels and are unable to exert downward price pressure.

6. European self-publishers experience some disadvantages to publishing via Kindle Direct Publishing. Amazon pays them more slowly, they must get clearance from the IRS or 30% of their income is withheld, and they are often taxed twice on their earnings. Amazon also pays lower royalty rates on many European sales, and European publishers are barred from certain US sales channels. As such, there are few non-English language e-books available, which reduces price competition and affects e-reader adoption rates.

There are four European Amazon sites: Italy, France, Germany and the UK, but only the latter two sell e-books, and only to customers in those countries. The rest must order from the US site, but some titles are restricted (based on which territorial rights the publisher owns).

United Kingdom

The UK is about a year behind the American e-book market. They have their own dedicated Kindle store, and it's very easy for UK authors to sell their e-books in the US market and vice versa. While Apple has made moves into the market, Kindles are still selling well enough to retain their position as the preferred e-reader, although Amazon itself is losing market share.

In the latest available figures, by the end of 2010 e-books had captured 6% of the UK publishing market, a growth of 300% on 2009. Bucking the trend noted in the US, Children's and Young Adult fiction grew faster still, posting gains of 500%.

Printed books in the United Kingdom are taxed at a zero-rate, but e-books are taxed at 20%. There have been moves to reduce the tax on digital work, but no legislation has been adopted to date. While this high tax rate is affecting sales of e-books, growth is speeding up and a surge in e-book numbers is expected in the lead-up to Christmas 2011.

Since the abolition of the Net Book Agreement—a fixed-price agreement between British publishers and retailers—supermarkets such as Tesco have become huge players in book-selling, and a lot of book-buying has moved online, which has led to the closure of several UK chains and existing chains diversifying into other, non-book products. Waterstone's, the largest book chain in the UK, has been in financial trouble for some time, and even independent bookstores are under constant threat of closure.

The Office of Fair Trading, a UK government body, is currently investigating the Agency Agreement to rule on whether or not it is illegal. If it does so, Amazon will be free to discount the price of e-books as much as it likes, selling at a loss if it chooses to, which will result in a huge depression in UK e-book prices, and an increase in Amazon's UK market share.

Ireland

The Irish market tends to follow the UK. Most successful Irish authors are published by UK (or US) publishing houses, have UK agents, and sell around 80% of their books there. Irish bookstores stock a significant range of Irish-published and Irish-interest books, but foreign titles still make up the majority of sales. VAT on e-books is 21% and is scheduled to rise to 23% by 2014. Although there is currently a zero-rate on print books, there are plans to abolish this and raise it to 23%.

France

France is slightly behind the UK in e-book numbers, and Apple is on track to capture a significant portion of the French e-reader market. French VAT on print books is 5.5% and the rate for e-books is 19.6%, although there is a proposal to reduce this to the lower rate in 2012.

The French parliament recently passed a law preventing retailers from discounting e-book prices by more than 5% of list price (which is set by the publishers). In a linked move, French publishers have banded together to create their own e-book retailing site. Whether this will be able to capture significant market share is doubtful.

At the beginning of March, the European Commission raided the offices of several French publishers under suspicion of e-book price-fixing. However, it has long been law in France (as well as Italy, Germany, and Spain) to fix the prices of print books. The EU has since announced that the investigation has expanded to several countries.

Germany

The respective tax rates for books in Germany are 7% on printed books and 19% on e-books. The German e-book market only accounted for 5.4% of sales in 2010, but the world's third-largest book market is expected to have a breakthrough in 2011, with 40,000 titles now available. Smaller publishers have greater access to the market in Germany and have seen strong growth in digital sectors.

Italy and Spain

Until mid-2010, there wasn't even an e-book market in Italy and Spain to track. Spain levies a 4% tax on print books and 18% on e-books. The government is attempting to bring in a standardized tax rate of 5.5% for all books. The Spanish-language market has huge potential, as it encompasses Spain, Mexico, Central America, and most of South America. Spain's Big Three publishers have announced a common platform to sell e-books.

Italy's tax rates on print books and e-books are 4% and 20% respectively. The Italian market is very small, with only about 7,000 titles available. Italian publishers have come together to provide a common retail site where customers can purchase e-books. While growth over Christmas was 400%, this was from an extremely low base.

In both markets, smartphones are popular and are the e-readers of choice.

The Future

Amazon may have missed a trick in Europe by officially only launching the Kindle in the UK and Germany. The Spanish-language market, for one, has huge potential.

The absence of Amazon as a major player has allowed Apple to make inroads with the iPad and the iPhone, and smartphones in general are poised to be big players in certain markets. Kobo has also made big moves and already has locally-merchandised English-language stories available in Canada, the UK, Hong Kong, New Zealand, and Australia. International versions of their wireless e-reader will soon be available across Europe. In July 2011, Kobo launched a store in Germany (with three times more local-language titles than Amazon), which will be followed by more in the Netherlands, Spain, France, and Italy.

While VAT rates have slowed growth across Europe, growth is still occurring, and speeding up, in all markets, and pressure is beginning to emerge to reduce the high tax rate on e-books.

European publishers have had extra time to prepare for these changes, but they haven't used it wisely. There is a huge fear of piracy amongst European publishers, but instead of combating this with cheap e-books that are easy to purchase, they have restricted access to the market by shutting out small publishers, have been slow to bring out digital versions, and have fixed high prices.

In short, they have doubled down on all the mistakes US publishers have made, even *without* Amazon breathing down their necks.

Appendix C—Practicalities

First of all, the legal stuff and a quick disclaimer. I am not a lawyer or an accountant, so none of this section, or indeed this entire book, should be considered legal advice, tax advice or anything like it. It is merely a starting point for you to conduct your own further investigations into tax and copyright laws relating to your country of residence.

Copyright

Now that the disclaimer is out of the way, the first thing you need to understand is that there is a difference between "publishing rights" and "copyright." If you sell a story to a magazine, or a book to a publisher, you are not usually assigning them the copyright. Rather, you are granting them *some* of the rights you have under copyright for the period defined in the contract, usually meaning they can publish and sell your work under certain conditions.

Open a trade published novel and flick to the copyright page. The book is still copyrighted in the author's name, usually in the form you see from my copyright notice (the year is the date of first publication): Copyright © 2011 David Gaughran

As for the rest of your notice, you can choose whatever wording you like. If you want, you can copy the notice from my page. You have my permission. (Don't forget to insert your own name rather than mine, you don't want all those royalty cheques heading my way.)

Copyright Law

Copyright law varies from country to country. The information included here is for the US, but there are links in the *Resources* section for other countries.

Your work is copyrighted as soon as it is tangible. In other words, once it makes its way out of your brain and onto the page (or even a computer screen), it is copyrighted. You might hear of writers posting a manuscript to themselves to ensure they are protected—this is known as "poor man's copyright" and it's a myth. It doesn't afford you any additional protection under the law. Your work is copyrighted as soon as you commit it to paper or pixel.

You will also hear people talk about "registering" copyright, which is optional but advisable. Registering your work will grant you additional rights and allow you to, among other things, sue for greater damages if someone plagiarizes your work. It costs $35 to register your copyright online in the US (go to www.copyright.gov), but even if you don't register your copyright, your work is still protected and you can still post a copyright notice at the front of your manuscript. You should note that the additional protections from registering your copyright in the US will only be afforded to US writers.

Another myth, especially among novice writers, is that they should register the copyright of their work before submitting it to an agent or editor. Let me be clear: a reputable agent or editor is *not* going to steal your story, and you shouldn't be submitting to any other kind. Registering your copyright before submitting can't hurt, but will serve only to mark you as an amateur.

Some people worry about their *ideas* being stolen. Let me also stop that one in its tracks. Experienced writers will all tell you the same thing: ideas are ten-a-penny. The art, and the sweat, is in the execution. To learn more about copyright law (and every writer really should), get yourself a copy of

The Copyright Handbook by Stephen Fishman.

Creative Commons

Even if you decide to give work away for free via creative commons, you should still attach a copyright notice to it that protects others profiting from your efforts.

You might want to consider a Creative Commons License, which doesn't alter any of your rights under copyright law but is an addition to them that instructs users in how they may share, amend, or use your document. There are many different licenses, with various restrictions. This book, for example, is able to be copied, shared, printed, and e-mailed, but not amended or used for commercial purposes. Attaching a Creative Commons License does not preclude you from exercising commercial rights. You can learn more about all the different kinds of licenses at: creativecommons.org

ISBN

A quick primer: ISBN stands for International Standard Book Number and is a unique code that identifies, among other things, the publisher of the book. You will recognize it as a string of 13 numbers sometimes seen on the title page of a book near the copyright notice or, more obviously, printed, along with a corresponding bar code, on the back of print versions.

Authors need to purchase an ISBN to publish a print book, but don't necessarily need one to publish an e-book. Amazon does not require an ISBN for e-books published through KDP, as they assign their own unique tracking code. The same goes for Barnes & Noble's digital publishing arm, PubIt.

An ISBN is required to publish with some of the other

retailers, like Sony and Apple; however, Smashwords are able to assign a free one if publishing to those distribution channels through them. If you opt for the free ISBN Smashwords offers, they will be identified as the publisher of your book on these sales channels. If that's a problem for you, they also sell individual ISBNs to US customers for $9.95. You also have the option of assigning your own ISBN (which you can also do when uploading to Amazon).

There are some self-publishers—usually those who put in all the hard yards prior to the rise of e-books—who think you aren't a *real* self-publisher unless you own your ISBN. I don't agree with that, but if you want your own ISBNs, for whatever reason, or if you are planning print versions of your book, then go ahead and purchase some.

Bowker is the only official source of ISBNs in the US and sells only to US writers (for links, and for other countries, please see *Resources*). A single ISBN costs $125 (although some authorized resellers charge $99), a block of 10 is $250, a block of 100 is $575, and a block of 1000 is $1000. The system is clearly tilted towards larger publishers. Obviously, most self-publishers, no matter how prolific, will not get through 1000 ISBNs.

You might be tempted to share a larger block of ISBNs with a group of other writers—don't be. They are non-transferable, so the original purchaser will be officially registered as the publisher of your book.

I haven't purchased any, as this is an expense that can be avoided. I don't see the advantage of adding one to my Amazon listings and I'm happy to use the free version from Smashwords. If having Smashwords listed as your publisher bothers you, you can always spend $9.95 and get your own if you are in the US. When I expand into print versions of my work, I will purchase ISBNs, but I'm not purchasing any for digital editions. You should note that you must have separate ISBNs for hardback, paperback, and digital editions, and that your free Smashwords ISBN cannot be used for any other edition.

Setting Up Your Own Publishing Company

Establishing your own company is by no means imperative; it's a personal decision. I publish all of my books through my company, Arriba Arriba Books. At the moment, the company doesn't have a website and the domain redirects to my blog. In the future, I may set up a website and possibly sell my books directly through it, but for now, it's just a name. I don't intend to publish any other writers through this company (and authors should think very carefully before going down that road); it's just for me.

If you decide to set up your own publishing company, there are a range of corporate structures you can use, and I can't give blanket advice as to which is most appropriate. It will depend on your own personal circumstances. Just make yourself aware of all of the regulatory and filing requirements in your particular country/state, as well as all of the tax implications.

Of course, you don't need to set up a company at all. You can just publish through your own name. But again, consult an accountant or tax professional about the relevant tax implications, which vary from country to country, and state to state.

Tax and International Writers

Amazon, Smashwords, and the other retailers are obliged to withhold 30% of an author's royalties unless they are provided with a Social Security Number (which only US or US-based writers will be able to do). They will hold onto this money until an author is able to clear his or her tax status with them, but only until the end of the tax year. After that, the money will be passed to the IRS. International authors can still apply to get the money back—it just becomes more hassle, so it's best to take care of it sooner rather than later. (Please note that you cannot file tax forms with the IRS until you have actually published.)

To claim it back, you must obtain an International Taxpayer Identification Number (ITIN) from the IRS. You do that by filling out Form W-7. It's a bit of a pain, but you only have to do it once. US tax accountant (and small publisher) Christine Pinheiro has put together an excellent step-by-step guide here: bit.ly/ku5I8v

Appendix D—Resources

This section contains all of the resources mentioned earlier in the book, as well as additional websites (and some books) you may find useful. Where necessary, I have added a brief explanation.

To get a handle on the current state of the publishing industry, I recommend reading from as many sources of as possible, including those you don't agree with. This is a time of great change in publishing. You should challenge your assumptions regularly to ensure your decisions are not skewed by outdated beliefs or faulty logic. Remember to also challenge the assumptions of those you regularly listen to. Everyone has a stake, and their opinions may be colored by that—something to keep in mind.

I won't highlight any of these resources in particular, other than to say that reading the last three or four years of Joe Konrath's blog and Dean Wesley Smith's blog is like a free Master's Degree in digital publishing, and keeping a close eye on Robin Sullivan's blog and Passive Guy's blog will make sure you don't miss a trick. There's probably a further 20 blogs I forgot to put in, and plenty more I don't know about yet. I highlight new ones every week on my own blog: davidgaughran.wordpress.com

Publishing Industry Blogs

Joe Konrath: jakonrath.blogspot.com
Dean Wesley Smith: deanwesleysmith.com
Robin Sullivan: write2publish.blogspot.com
Passive Guy: thepassivevoice.com

Kris Rusch: kriswrites.com
Michael Stackpole: michaelastackpole.com
Mike Shatzkin: idealog.com

Trade Publishing Magazines

The Bookseller (UK): thebookseller.com
GalleyCat: mediabistro.com/galleycat
E-Book Newser: mediabistro.com/ebooknewser
Publishers Weekly: publishersweekly.com

Literary Agent Blogs

Kristin Nelson: pubrants.blogspot.com
Rachelle Gardner: rachellegardner.com
Miss Snark (Archives): misssnark.blogspot.com

Editor Blogs

Alan Rinzler: alanrinzler.com/blog
Tom Dupree: tomdup.wordpress.com
Pimp My Novel: pimpmynovel.blogspot.com
Karin Cox: karincox.wordpress.com

Self-publishing Advice

Kindle Boards Writers' Café: kindleboards.com

Writing Advice

On Writing by Stephen King
Self-editing for Fiction Writers by Renni Brown & Dave King
Margo Lerwill: urbanpsychopomp.blogspot.com
Sommer Leigh: sommerleigh.com

Nathan Bransford: forums.nathanbransford.com
Absolute Write: absolutewrite.com/forums

Writer Beware

This is an excellent free service provided by the SWFA, which, among other things, warns against scam agents, unscrupulous publishers, and inexperienced or unprofessional editors.
Website: sfwa.org/for-authors/writer-beware
Blog: accrispin.blogspot.com

Background Checks

Absolute Write has a comprehensive sub-forum called "Bewares, Recommendations & Background Check" which has separate threads on most editors, publishers, literary agents, and those who provide writers' services, sharing other writer's experiences. If the company in question is not listed there, you can post about it, and someone will answer you. Check the background of anyone you deal with.
Absolute Write: bit.ly/nH4ZhM

Book Design/Covers

My page: davidgaughran.wordpress.com/covers/
Book Cover Archive: bookcoverarchive.com
The Book Designer: www.thebookdesigner.com

Read E-books on Your Phone or Computer

Free Kindle Apps (to read MOBI files): amzn.to/jJr1CU
Free Nook Apps (to read EPUB files): bit.ly/pqvphb

E-book Formatting

Guido Henkel's peerless guide: bit.ly/qjjBKR
My guide: bit.ly/oNAe1n
Smashwords Style Guide: bit.ly/nqFLO3

Free Formatting Software

HTML Editor (PC): notepad-plus-plus.org
HTML Editor (Mac): bit.ly/qoG8MM
E-book Converter (PC & Mac): calibre-ebook.com

Formatting Services

If you insist on paying for your formatting, these services are
consistently recommended, and charge reasonable rates.
Guido Henkel: bit.ly/qcK2gm
Rob Siders: 52novels.com

Blurb Copywriting

Publetariat: bit.ly/puaFxa

Blogging

The College of Blogging: bit.ly/oBVsg5

Twitter Advice

Michael Hicks: bit.ly/pzDyfj

Designing Your Facebook Page

Technipedia: bit.ly/pvlbjb

Reviewer Lists

Review sites are opening (and closing) all the time. Please check my blog for an updated list or the Kindle Boards forum.
Simon Royle's List: bit.ly/o42vB2
Christine Pinheiro's List: bit.ly/nF0qe1

Sales Tracking

NovelRank: novelrank.com
Titlez: titlez.com

Podcasting

Podiobooks: podiobooks.com

Readers Forums/Websites

Kindle Boards: kindleboards.com
Nook Boards: nookboards.com/forum
KU Forum (UK): kuforum.co.uk
Mobileread: mobileread.com
LibraryThing: librarything.com
Goodreads: goodreads.com
For an example of how to use a reader's forum effectively, so that you aren't chased out for spamming the users, please read this blog post: bit.ly/oud9Yu

Copyright

The Copyright Handbook by Stephen Fishman
US: copyright.gov
Canada: bit.ly/quG0OM
UK: bit.ly/oNhm6z
Ireland: cai.ie
Australia: copyright.org.au

ISBNs

US: bit.ly/oqFihX
Canada: bit.ly/pC3y9g
UK & Ireland: bit.ly/qzqigx
Australia: bit.ly/opfPZ1

Tax

Getting an ITIN: bit.ly/ku5I8v

Acknowledgements

I would like to thank my editor, Karin Cox, pleonasm-hunter par excellence. She took an active role in shaping this book and was an excellent sounding board throughout. Any remaining errors are due to my own stubbornness or intransigence. Kate Gaughran, once again, has come up with a stunning cover by not listening to me and doing things her way. And Heather Adkins did a lovely job on the print edition.

This idea grew organically from my blog. But without my blog-readers—who hunted down typos with zeal (and a special mention for JJ Toner and Holly Grant), who continued the debate in the comments, and who gave support and encouragement at every turn—this book would be all the poorer. I would also like to thank all of the bloggers in the self-publishing world. I learned everything in these pages from you. Thank you for your generosity and openness.

My contributors deserve a special thank you. They took time out of their extremely busy schedules to contribute their stories to this book. Cheryl Shireman, Victorine Lieske, Michael Hicks, CJ Archer, Beth Orsoff, Bob Mayer, Debora Geary, Sibel Hodge, Consuelo Saah Baehr, Steven Hawk, Suzanne Tyrpak, Mel Comley, Jason Letts, Melanie Nilles, Jan Hurst-Nicholson, KC May, Terri Reid, Gerald Hawksley, N Gemini Sasson, Susanne O'Leary, Mark Williams, Shayne Parkinson, Stacey Wallace Benefiel, Sarah Woodbury, Kenneth Rosenberg, Katie Klein, Nell Gavin, Martin C. Sharlow, William Esmont, Lexi Revellian, J Carson Black, Imogen Rose, and Mark Edwards, you deserve all of your success and more.

   I would like to thank my family and friends for their endless support and their continuous help. Finally, I want to say something to my wife-to-be, Ivča Vostrovska. Thank you for taking the leap with me. I don't know where we're going to end up, but I promise it will be fun along the way.

About the Author

David Gaughran is a 33-year old Irish writer, living in Sweden, who spends most of his time traveling the world, collecting stories. *A Storm Hits Valparaíso* is his debut novel, but he is the author of several short stories and a popular guide to digital self-publishing. To sign up to his new-release mailing list, please visit this link: bit.ly/valpolist.

A Storm Hits Valparaíso. Catalina Flores de la Peña's tongue got her in more trouble than any other part of her body, even though there were far more likely candidates. But when a storm rolls into her sleepy port town, she finds herself embroiled with a gang of adventurers, mercenaries, and prostitutes on a journey to free South America from the Spanish Empire.

A Storm Hits Valparaíso is an epic historical adventure starring two brothers torn apart by love; a slave running for his life; a disgraced British sailor seeking redemption; and José de San Martín, an Argentine general who deserts the Spanish Army to lead a bloody revolt against his former masters.

"David Gaughran has woven a captivating story set during this dangerous period in South America's history. I'd happily recommend it to fans of the genre." — Tracy Cook, *Booked Up Reviews.*

"Gaughran assembles a multi-national cast of characters in an ambitious story of love and betrayal, sea and land battles, victory and defeat in a war for independence. In characters drawn from real historical figures, the author delves into the politics of war and how battles turn on the smallest of details or the whims of a single man."—J.W. Manus

"A work of sweeping historical fiction that captivates and entertains ... engaging and richly textured."—John Glass

"A romping classico... it reminded me of Louis de Bernières."—Stuart Noss

There is a sample at the end of this book, and the e-book is available from the web-store of Arriba Arriba Books - bit.ly/DGebooks - and all major retailers. The paperback edition is available from Amazon, Barnes & Noble, and The Book Depository (free worldwide shipping). All of the following titles are currently only available as e-books, but don't forget you can read e-books on any computer, tablet, laptop, or smartphone with this free app from Amazon: amzn.to/jJr1CU.

If You Go Into The Woods, a collection of two creepy short stories for $0.99, is available from the web-store of Arriba Arriba Books - bit.ly/DGebooks - and all major retailers. The title story was chosen to appear in the *Short Story America Anthology, Volume 1*, a collection of their best stories of the past year, published June 2011. The other—*The Reset Button*—is published for the first time in any format.

"A fine story that looms in the mind of the reader long after the last page ... aspirational fiction, the kind of magic realism that reads deliciously, but like a delicate soufflé, is a difficult feat to pull off."—Matt Ellis, author of *Strange As Angels* and *Lumpen*.

"There are definite shades of HP Lovecraft in both stories ... punchy, entertaining reads with a bit of mental gymnastics thrown in, you can't go wrong with this one."—Jenny Mounfield, *The Compulsive Reader*, author of *The Ice-cream Man*.

"Two very well-constructed and thought-provoking tales from an author I know I will be keeping my eyes on. 4.5 stars."—Heather L. Faville, *Doubleshot Reviews*.

"This is the most professional design—both inside and

out—that I have seen since I started reviewing at *SIFT*. The writing in this story is top-notch. The writer has a strong, clean voice. He's able to sustain an air of mystery and suspense without it feeling cheap."—Sarah Nicolas, *SIFT Book Reviews.*

"I heartily recommend this masterful piece of work to any and all that thoroughly enjoy the art of the word, and especially to those that have a special place in their hearts for short stories, as I believe this to be a fabulous exponent of the genre."—LE Olteano, *Butterfly Books*

Transfection is another short story, but this time with an old-school science fiction vibe. It's also available for $0.99 from the web-store of Arriba Arriba Books - bit.ly/DGebooks - and all major retailers.

"I laughed out loud at some of the antics as I was reading. Transfection is well worth the price-tag ... yet another well written and, dare I say again, thought-provoking, tale from David Gaughran."—Heather L. Faville, *Doubleshot Reviews.*

"Well written ... a polished product."—TC, *Booked Up Reviews.*

"Very strong images ... a haunting quality ... I totally did not expect that ending. I really didn't see it coming ... I recommend this to people who enjoy well written sci-fi."— LE Olteano, *Butterfly Books.*

Say Hello:

David Gaughran blogs about writing and the book business every day. He would love it if you dropped by to say hello: davidgaughran.wordpress.com

He also runs *South Americana*, which shares curious incidents from the history of the world's most exotic continent: www.SouthAmericana.com

Alternatively, send him an email –
david.gaughran@gmail.com –
or follow him on Twitter: twitter.com/DavidGaughran

Word-of-mouth is crucial for any author to succeed. If you enjoyed the book, please consider leaving a review on Amazon (or any other site), even if it's only a line or two; it would make all the difference and would be very much appreciated.

Amazon US: amzn.to/sgDzkH
Amazon UK: amzn.to/vDzIvG

A Storm Hits Valparaíso (Sample)

Catalina Flores de la Peña's tongue got her in more trouble than any other part of her body, even though there were far more likely candidates. However, as soon as anyone brought these to her attention, they realized why most men preferred to admire her from the dusty corners of her father's tavern, rather than approach her directly. So legendary was her temper that the mayor ordered her father to keep her upstairs when dignitaries came to visit the tavern, fearing a repeat of the night she broke the magistrate's nose.

When she was confined to her room, customers tended not to linger; there was no one to hasten the hours between the first *pisco* and the fall of night. Watching her glide between tables—flirting with one man, berating another, eyes flashing one moment, soft and kind the next—was one of the more pleasant ways to avoid thinking about the weather on Valparaíso's long winter nights.

Her father—Don Flores—was a stern man and no one was quite sure of his first name. One customer swore his uncle grew up with Don Flores in Pucon, and that he was called Ignacio. Another insisted his brother once loitered outside the confessional and heard old Father Guido refer to Don Flores as Ricardo. Catalina's father never let on, happy to give the men something to talk about other than his daughter. And anyway, the majority of his patrons were content simply calling him Don Flores, the honorific reflecting the distance he kept from them.

Don Flores' low opinion of his fellow man resulted from years of seeing them at their worst, for he slept when he wasn't working and he worked when he wasn't sleeping. His daughter was spared this judgment. He showered her with all the love and affection he withheld from the rest of society. When Catalina was old enough, he insisted she work at the bar so that she would form the same useful opinion of humanity that protected and comforted him in equal measure.

* * *

Catalina could feel his eyes—watching her. She tried to ignore him, but every time she looked, there he was. Most men had the decency to look away when she caught them, but this Spanish *puerco* just went on staring, with the faintest hint of a sneer at the corner of his lips.

Something about him kept her on edge. She tried to put him out of her mind; she had troubles enough tonight. The crew of the *Esmeralda* had descended on Valparaíso with no good in mind. Their ship had docked, needing repairs, and they were taking advantage of several days of unexpected shore leave before continuing on to Lima. It had been a long voyage from Spain. The sailors hadn't seen port during the journey across the Atlantic, down the barren coast of Patagonia, past the frozen wastelands of Tierra del Fuego, and around Cape Horn into the Pacific. The Chilean rebels had no ships worthy of the name, and their forces had withdrawn on sight of the frigate; their one paltry cannon was no match for the *Esmeralda's* forty-two guns. The Spaniards had secured the waterfront in under an hour, encountering no resistance. Sentries were posted at each street corner, and the sailors who escaped guard duty were determined to make the most of this opportunity.

Toward midnight, the bawdy crowd began to clear, following the musicians down the street, looking for whores and gambling tables. An hour later, only one table was left: Spanish sailors, drunk, shouting insults. Except for him; he just watched. She tried to shake it off, hoping they would be gone soon. Instead, they called for another drink.

"Very well, *señores*," said Don Flores, as he poured the *pisco*, "one more, then we close."

Catalina placed the drinks on the table, grateful the night was nearly over, already thinking of bed. As she turned to leave, the *puerco* grabbed her arm. "I hope you are not going to throw us out on the street just yet. It's still early."

Catalina glared at him. "Let go of me, *puerco*, or you'll be out now."

He pulled her down onto his lap, grabbing her breast. "*Chica*, the night's only beginning—" He stopped short, her cold metal blade pressed against his throat. The bar fell silent—a silence quickly shattered by his companions jumping up from their chairs, upending the table in their haste. Catalina pulled the *puerco's* head back, exposing his sweaty neck. One of the sailors edged closer. The tip of her dagger nicked the *puerco's* skin, drawing a small bead of blood.

"Stand back lads," he cautioned.

Catalina turned to his companions. "You two, leave."

They paused. The *puerco* gave a slight nod, the knife still firmly at his neck. Eyes on Catalina, his companions staggered backward to the door and stepped outside. Her father hurried to her side and eased the knife from her fingers. With his other hand, he twisted the *puerco's* arm up behind his back and marched him after his companions.

"You tell that bitch this isn't finished." The *puerco* struggled. "I'll be back for her."

Don Flores threw him out the door, bolting it shut. He sighed then looked at his daughter. "Go to bed *mi hija*. It has been a long night. Tomorrow we can clean."

Catalina nodded and went upstairs.

The next morning, the air thick with stale sweat and tobacco, Catalina drummed her fingers on the bar as she surveyed the damage. *This day isn't going to improve in a hurry*, she thought. Last night's crowd had been rough. Aside from dirty glasses and plates, she had smashed bottles and broken chairs to contend with. At least her regulars knew the rules—and occasionally respected them—but those animals, they

3

had no respect for anything. She cursed as a glass slipped from her hand and shattered. A groan came from the doorway outside. *Pedro*, she thought, a smile sailing through the storm of her face.

Every night, Pedro Villar fell asleep in the doorway of the bar with a flower in his hand, intending to profess his love to Catalina. Every night, his courage would falter, leaving him slumped outside, cursing his cowardice and mourning his solitude. Every morning, Catalina sent him home to his mother—a stern woman who put a raw egg in his coffee as punishment for his nightly excesses.

Catalina opened the door and shooed Pedro away with the broom, unmindful of the heart she broke a little more each day.

"Pedro Villar?" Her father appeared as she was re-locking the door.

Catalina laughed. "Who else?"

"He has too much interest in you for my liking."

"That drunk would chase a *burro* in a dress."

Her father grunted. "Catalina, put down that broom. I want to talk to you."

"What is it, Papa?"

"I'm sending you to Santiago for a few days, to your aunt. I don't want any argument. It's not safe for you here."

"But Papa, we can't let—"

"Sergeant Eduardo came by last night, after you went to bed. He is worried about these sailors. They are hot-headed and foolish enough to do something stupid." Don Flores took a bottle of *pisco* from the shelf, cleaning the label with his thumb before pouring himself a healthy measure. "He can't protect us. His hands are tied. None of his men can enter Valparaíso while there is a Spanish warship in the bay." He emptied the contents with one gulp. "He feels it would be best if you visited some relatives until the Spaniards leave town."

"But this is my home."

"I have made my decision, Catalina. Just for a few days,

until these sailors leave." He raised his hands, as if to brook any further discussion.

"Papa—"

"That's enough!"

Catalina continued cleaning in silence. There was no point arguing; her father's mind was made up. She had no siblings to share the burden of her father's protectiveness, no mother to soften his resolve; she was going to Santiago.

* * *

A Storm Hits Valparaíso is available in paperback from Amazon and as an e-book from Amazon, Barnes & Noble, Apple, Smashwords, Kobo, and Sony.

Made in the USA
Charleston, SC
13 July 2012